How to Multiply Your Money
a beginner's guide to futures/options trading

How to Multiply Your Money
a beginner's guide to futures/options trading

by
Merrill J. Oster
with
Darrell Jobman
Sherman L. Levin
Mike Walsten
Paul Wilcox

"There are few investments in the world
that can have the multiplying effect on your money
found in commodity speculation."

Investor Publications
Box 6, Cedar Falls, Iowa 50613

Published by Investor Publications, Inc.
Box 6
Cedar Falls, Iowa 50613

First Edition, 1979
SECOND EDITION, 1981
Third Edition, 1985

Library of Congress Cataloging in Publication Data

Oster, Merrill J., 1940-
    How to Multiply your Money . . . a Beginner's Guide to
    Commodity Speculation

    Bibliography: p. 209
    Includes index
    1. Commodity exchanges. I. Title.
HG6046.08   332.6'44   78-14888
ISBN 0-914230-03-4

About the Authors

Merrill Oster

Publisher of *Futures* magazine, president of Professional Farmers of America. Merrill writes from more than a decade of personal experience in futures trading. His global view of market forces and detailed understanding of how futures markets work help you understand the real world of futures and options.

Darrell Jobman

Editor of *Futures* magazine. Darrell's broad perspective of the futures and options industry sharpen this book's description of how successful traders operate.

Sherman L. Levin

Author of the widely-respected *Market Interpreter.* He is a consultant to the government, exchanges and grain trade on trading techniques and strategies after serving as research director for a major brokerage firm and a major grain company. He has unique knowledge of world financial and economic trends.

Mike Walsten

Editorial director of Professional Farmers of America and editor of *PorkPro* newsletter. Mike's seasoned experience with the major farm commodities puts perspective around basic charting techniques.

Paul Wilcox

Market analyst and editor of two weekly technical services: *Commodity Price Charts* and *Commodity Closeup.* Paul trades personally and is the chief technical analyst of Professional Farmers of America. He maintains minute-by-minute touch with the futures market.

Foreword

I know the "thrill of victory" in commodity trading — a $20,000 profit from a one-day market move. But when you make that kind of money, you assume huge risks. That's why I have also experienced the "agony of defeat" — watching $20,000 pour out the window in a single day. On balance, the futures market has coughed up substantial gains to my account. But the final chapter is not written for any commodity trader until he closes out his last trade.

Most traders who have tasted a little success don't want to quit, even after they are far ahead. Commodity trading is exciting. The excitement goes far beyond the obvious potential for substantial financial gains.

The commodity speculator, much like the properly-motivated professional athlete, presses on for the sheer challenge of victory. Just as in professional baseball, if in your pursuit you achieve excellence, financial success follows.

The odds of becoming a successful speculator are much greater than the odds of a sandlotter becoming a New York Yankee.

Commodity trading requires discipline. An undisciplined commodity trader who makes impetuous, bull-headed trades is destined to the minor leagues of trading success just as surely as the short stop who overindulges in ice cream and candy.

This book gives beginning traders an overview of how commodity trading works. Some traders never get to first base because they don't understand the game's fundamentals. They take unnecessary risks and engage in trades which have a high chance of failure.

Hopefully, this book will help put the odds of success on your side.

Learn the fundamentals first. That rule is as important in money management as in sports. The fine points come easier later. This is a book on basics. For that reason, it will be helpful for the beginner as well as the experienced trader who wants to review the basics.

Commodity trading is like baseball in one other very important respect. You don't have to hit a home run every time to be successful in baseball or commodity futures trading. A .300 hitter in commodity trading (three successful trades in ten) can become a millionaire if his losing trades generate small losses and his winners generate large gains. But that lofty goal is achieved only by the well-disciplined trader.

If you use the basics in this book to develop trading discipline, you're on your way. Success won't happen overnight. I stumbled along for seven years having just enough good months to keep me coming back. Losses those first seven years were $3,000 to $5,000 per year. Then I learned how to apply the technical tools discussed in Chapters 8 through 10. My most recent seven years of trading have been profitable. I have combined the fundamentals in Chapter 7 and the technical aspects in Chapters 8 through 10 to greatly improve my timing skills.

I offer you no secret formula. No hot broker. No magic wand. Just some common sense basics that have helped me. This book is just a starter. Obviously, you need a continual flow of information as a commodity trader. (See Chapter 15.)

Your broker may be an excellent market source; however, good and timely research appears to be available only for the high commission, large accounts. And my associates through *Futures* magazine and *Commodity Price Charts* provide timely information for commodity traders. We hope to be of service to you for years to come.

Merrill J. Oster, Publisher
Futures magazine
Cedar Falls, Iowa

Table of Contents

Dawn . . . Head-and-Shoulders Bottom: Old Reliable . . . Flags, Pennants, Coils Point the Way . . . Triangles Yield Objectives, too

1
Why People Speculate in Futures

Futures speculation is one of the few ways you can multiply a small bankroll into a small fortune in a short time. A $2,000 investment usually buys one $100,000 contract of T-bonds. You double your money if the price goes up two full points. Moves of that size take place in the futures market nearly every week.

The main difference between trading futures and stocks is that each $1 invested in the stock market controls $2 worth of stock, if you buy on margin. But, each $1 in the futures market frequently controls $20 worth of commodities. That's the ultimate in financial leverage. In addition, price fluctuations usually are greater in futures than stocks. That's why there are opportunities for much quicker profits and losses in futures trading.

Because your $1 controls $20 of someone else's money, futures trading is also one of the few places where you can turn a large fortune into a small one and fast. Financial losers outnumber winners more than 2 to 1, according to an industry survey. But the futures speculator has the attitude, "Losers outnumber the true winners by 2 to 1 in many businesses. Because winners in futures trading are frequently big winners, it's worth the risk."

It's the Bulls vs. the Bears

Futures speculators risk their capital believing they can properly anticipate price changes. There is no guarantee of profits. They "speculate" on the probability of price moves, hence the label "speculators."

Speculators who believe the market is heading higher are "bulls." They are "bullish" on a commodity because, for one or more reasons, they believe prices are headed higher. They profit by buying at today's prices and selling at a higher price later.

If a specualtor believes prices are headed lower, the trade calls him a "bear." A bear makes his money by selling a commodity at the current price and buying it back later at a lower price.

The constant tug-of-war and differences of opinion between the bulls and the bears are what makes a market. The daily closing price of a commodity is the level where the balance between the bulls and bears was reached in the final moments of trading. Closing prices and the daily ranges are the point of reference for the next day's trading.

Beginning traders quickly familiarize themselves with the market page of the local daily newspaper. It details the activity of the previous day's trade in most major futures contracts.

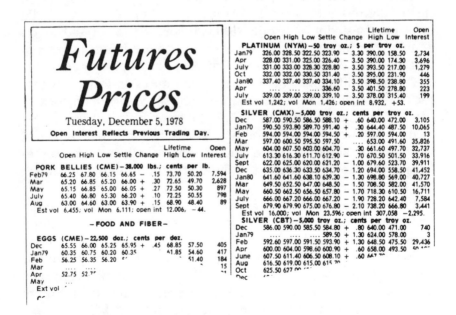

The Attitude of a Disciplined Trader

As a beginner in futures speculation, you naturally seek a good return on your money in a short period of time. Futures trading is not like stock trading or land buying where you expect to hold for several years for price appreciation. Futures trading is a short-term venture that often calls for quick reactions and is, therefore, not the type of speculation that fits everyone's psychological makeup.

The experts pass along one solid rule to the beginner: Put up only that cash which you are willing to lose.

If you trade with your grocery money, you become so emotionally attached to your money that it influences your ability to trade. There is always a chance you will take a position that will move against you immediately and wipe out your total equity. Because there is this chance, money put into the futures market must be considered nonessential funds, if you are to become a disciplined, unemotional futures trader.

You reduce your chance of losing all of your trading funds by carefully selecting the right trade. That is a topic for later chapters. There are also techniques such as "stop loss" orders which usually can get you out of the market before your equity is washed away in losses. Nevertheless, you must be prepared to lose it all, even though you hope for substantial gain. This attitude of having a willingness to lose your capital is vitally important if you are to become an objective trader.

How Much Risk Can You Afford?

Every person has his own unique risk-bearing ability. If you are one of the conservative types who is afraid to borrow money, chances are futures trading will provide a little too much financial excitement.

Trading in volumes and risk levels above your own comfort level reduces your ability to sleep at night. Each of us has a "comfort level." Your basic emotional makeup and financial values help determine what your comfort level is. No formula fits all traders, but it is important to note that just because someone you know is trading 10,000 bu. of soybeans is no reason for you to assume that risks this large might not give you an ulcer. Carefully assess your psychological comfort level before you enter the market.

It is easier to figure out how much risk you can afford from a financial point of view. Take a look at your financial statement. Line up your assets (things you own) in order of their ease of conversion to cash. Those assets that are easily converted to cash are termed "quick assets" or short-term assets. Do the same with your debts. Compare your short-term assets with your short-term liabilities (debts) and begin to play with the numbers. What would happen if you lost $5,000? Would you still have enough cash and income to service your remaining debt? How about $10,000? Could you handle a $10,000 loss and still meet your house payments, car payments, etc.?

Through a careful analysis of your current finances, you can arrive at your financial ability to carry risk. However, you might find you can afford to lose $5,000, but when you begin trading, you are so nervous about losing the $5,000 that you decide you aren't ready for the emotional risk of trading. In that case, back off and trade smaller risks within your comfort level.

What's the Minimum Capital Required?

Although a few successful traders have started with as little as $1,000 in their account, it is better to start with at least $5,000 of trading equity. Starting with less than $5,000 in your risk account pressures you to make correct decisions in your first few trades. You might be a .300 hitter (three profitable trades in ten), but if you can't afford the losses associated with the first three losing trades, you may be out of the game before you have a chance to close ten trades and hit three winners.

Risk-reward Ratio is High in Futures

In the not-too-recent past, inflation was everyone's consideration. If you put $5,000 in an insured savings account at 6% interest there was a very low risk of losing your capital; however, when there was double-digit inflation the risk was much larger. There is now mixed opinion as to whether there will be a return to inflation or if the United States economy has turned to deflation. If there is deflation, then the security and high interest rates (which is to say the return on your investment) have encouraged the purchase of government obligations. The fact that the economy presents the investor with the problem of deciding whether to handle his investments with either inflation or deflation in mind makes it clear that the prudent investor will return to the virtues of the past. He will, in fact, put the bulk of his capital in the safer investment category while limiting his exposure to the higher reward of higher risk opportunities.

You might seek something with a little more risk. Your money may earn 10% or 12% in "commercial paper" — a loan to a commercial company. Now the risk is a bit higher. There's always the chance the company which holds the commercial paper will go bankrupt. That's why the reward is a bit higher. . . the risk is higher, too.

Real estate carries an even higher risk. There is always the chance that you can't get any rental return on real estate. Because there is that risk, real estate investors hope for a 7% to 15% return on their capital.

At an even higher risk level, you might accept more risk and invest in common stocks. There is a chance of an economic slump. In that event, stocks you buy will be worth less than when you purchased them. For that reason, there must be a slightly higher reward to attract investment dollars. Some stock investors can lose it all; others earn 1,000% increases on their equity. The average annual return to stockholders, including appreciation and dividends, was about 9% from 1926 through 1960. Since then, years have been both substantially better and substantially worse than 9%.

Futures markets carry even higher risks and, therefore, even higher potential rewards. Successful traders aim at doubling their money in the market each year. That would be a 100% return. A 50% return would be an average year for the professional speculator. And many make that kind of return — occasionally. There's even the person who invests $10,000 and hits it big with a $1,000,000 profit in a year or two. But, those opportunities are rare.

Because there is a chance for big money in futures, there's also the chance for a quick, large loss. That's why, as a beginning trader, you must understand the risk before you start. Then, develop a trading plan that is consistent with your risk-bearing ability.

Why Futures Speculation Is So Attractive

You'll learn more about futures price charts and how to read them in later chapters, but the actual chart for December 1978 corn futures on the next page illustrates why futures trading is so appealing to the speculator seeking greater financial returns.

We'll assume that you were smart enough to buy a corn futures contract near the bottom around $2.45 per bu. in the first week of May. Note that prices trended up until the first of June. As the price

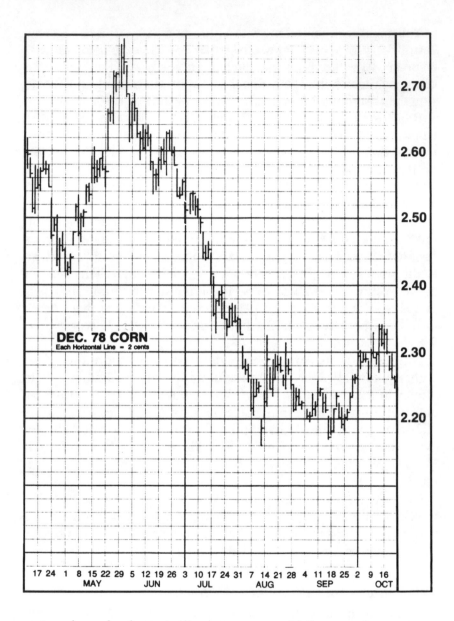

DEC. 78 CORN
Each Horizontal Line = 2 cents

uptrend was broken, we'll assume you sold the corn futures contract at $2.65 around June 5. Result: 20¢ per bu. profit for you, or $1,000 for the 5,000-bu. contract traded at the Chicago Board of Trade. For an initial minimum margin of $750 for a 5,000-bu. corn contract, you would have had a return of well over 100% after allowing for commissions — in just one month! Had you gotten out near the top at $2.75, you would have received another $500, or nearly a 200% return. But few traders are smart enough to pick tops and bottoms.

Substantial profits accumulate in futures accounts when prices are going down if the traders took a "short" position. Assume that when you got out of your original position, you sold an additional 5,000-bu. contract at $2.65 per bushel. That would make you net "short," or "bearish" in trade terminology. The chart shows how corn futures prices trended downward during the summer of 1978. As prices bottomed in late August, assume you bought back the futures contract around $2.30 per bushel. Result: 35¢ per bu. profit on your "short" position, or $1,750 for a 5,000-bu. contract. After commissions, that's a return of about 225% on the initial $750 margin money you must put up for each 5,000-bu. contract — in less than three months!

If you put the $1,000 profit on the "long" side together with the $1,750 profit on the "short" side, that's a return of $2,750, less commissions, on your initial $750 margin investment in just four months. Annualized, that's a return of well over 1,000%!

This is just an example with corn futures. T-Bills, gold and more than 50 other commodities can produce some even more astounding figures — and, in some cases, a lot more risk. Futures trading isn't as easy as presented here, of course. But it's the potential for big returns that attracts people to speculate in the futures market.

2
Who Uses Futures
Markets — the Players

Futures traders fall into two categories: hedgers and speculators. Hedgers are producers or users of commodities. Producers are farmers, ranchers, miners, etc., who grow or dig commodities that are vital to world trade. Users buy the raw commodities to process, transport, export, manufacture, etc. The ultimate user, of course, is the consumer.

Producers naturally attempt to get the top price for their commodity; users usually try to buy the commodity at the lowest possible price favorable to them. Like it or not, every producer and every user must face the risk of price change. For them, the key function of futures markets is to find someone to share some of the price risk they can't afford to take themselves.

They do so by buying and selling futures contracts. These contracts are exactly the same as a contract for the physical article, whether it be bushels of corn, Deutsche marks, or the dollar value of a stock index. The contract calls for the delivery of a certain amount of a certain quality of a named commodity at a specified destination at a certain time for an agreed-upon amount of money. A futures contract is the same thing, with all of the terms being agreed to in advance, except for the amount and price which is handled through public outcry in the pits.

The Role of the Speculator

Into this tug-of-war between producer-seller and user-buyer comes the speculator to serve as the vital link, the lubricant that makes futures markets work. The gambler creates risk by betting on a card or a horse, determining the amount of his risk by the size of his bets. The futures speculator, however, has a far different role. He assumes risk that already exists. He doesn't make risks. He picks up the risk a producer or user doesn't want. For his risk-bearing efforts, the speculator naturally hopes to gain from price changes.

To get an idea who uses futures markets and how they fit into the total picture, let's use a fictitious small-scale example at your local grocery store to illustrate how futures work.

Let's assume when you walk into the grocery store you see eggs priced at 50¢ per doz., a price you believe to be very reasonable. You obviously couldn't store 50 doz. eggs in your refrigerator for a year, so you tell the grocer, "I'd like to lock in a price for my eggs for the next year at 50¢ per dozen." The grocer says, "Come back tomorrow and I'll see what I can work out."

In the meantime, the grocer calls his farmer friend who currently supplies eggs to the store for 40¢ per dozen. "Jones, I have this egg customer who buys one doz. Grade A large eggs every week. He would like to lock in a price for the next year. I can't guarantee him a price unless you guarantee me a price. Will you write a contract for 50 doz. eggs, delivered one doz. per week for the next 50 weeks, at 40¢ per dozen?"

The farmer puzzles for a moment, looks at his corn crop, considers his hen numbers and decides his costs should remain about the same for the next year. "Yes, sir, I'll be more than happy to lock in that price. It guarantees me a profit and an outlet for 50 doz. eggs. I'll write up that contract."

The next day, you walk up to your grocer and he happily announces, "I've worked out a deal. You sign here and I'll sell you a doz. eggs every week for 50¢ per doz., regardless of what the price of eggs might do in the next 50 weeks."

Everyone Benefits From Futures Trading

You walk away happy. You can plan on a set price for eggs for the next year.

The farmer is happy. He has locked in his margin of profit for that 50 doz. eggs for the next year.

The grocer is happy. He has locked in a profit margin. There is no worry that falling market prices will wash away his profit.

This is an oversimplified version of the futures market. Someone guarantees to buy a certain amount of a commodity; someone guarantees to sell. The grocer is a simplified version of the middlemen, such as brokers, elevators, commodity exchanges, and others who facilitate the trade between buyer and seller.

Let's carry this example just a bit farther. Let's assume that shortly after you entered into your egg contract with the local broker, the price of eggs skyrocketed 50¢ higher to $1.00 per dozen! You tell the neighbors that you still are paying 50¢ per doz. for the eggs while they are paying $1.00 per dozen.

At that time, your neighbors read in the newspaper that there is a major chicken shortage in the world and that eggs might go to $2.00 per dozen. They run down to the grocery store and ask the grocer if he will sell them a contract of eggs at $1.00. By this time, the grocer has been flooded with requests. Other neighborhood businessmen see that owning an egg contract could have real profit potential for them.

How Speculators Multiply Their Money

Even though each family needs only 50 doz. eggs in the next year, some have purchased 10 contracts of eggs (500 doz.) hoping (speculating) that they either will sell the eggs at a higher price or sell their contract later at a higher price. For example, if they have a guaranteed price of $1.00 per doz. and the price of eggs goes to $2.00 per doz., that would be a profit of $50 on each 50-doz. contract. "With 10 contracts, I could make $500," reasons one of your neighbors.

With all of this interest in buying, the grocer has had to drum up some interest in selling egg contracts. Some egg producers don't believe the reports of a serious hen shortage. They know there have been more chicks hatched in the last 90 days than at any time in history, so they become willing sellers at $1.00 per dozen.

The only concern the grocer has is that someone who has purchased or sold a contract of 50 doz. eggs might not fulfill his agreement or might default on the contract. To prevent this from happening, he asks both the buyer and seller of the contract to put up 10% of the value of the contract as security. That 10% is put into a bank account and is held until the contract is executed.

The word now has spread all over the city about your smashing financial success. You purchased a contract of eggs for 50¢ per doz., and now eggs are selling for $1.00 per dozen. Your success has caused many speculators to come to the store and buy contracts in hopes of eggs going higher. But some speculators, like egg producers, believe prices are headed lower, so they are interested in selling a contract at $1.00 with the idea of buying eggs in the country at 50¢ to fulfill the delivery requirements of the contract at a later day. These speculators represent the "bears" who make a profit only when the market goes down.

Now, the grocer is so busy handling egg speculators, egg buyers (homemakers) and egg sellers (producers) that he must work almost full-time handling the contracts. Some people buy contracts, then sell the contracts to other people later, with no intention of making delivery of the eggs on the contract. These speculators are buying and selling in hopes of a quick profit from a short-term trade. But you hang onto your contract until the eggs actually are delivered, because you want them for your family.

Development of Futures Markets

This little grocery store example is not at all unlike the beginning of the first commodity futures exchanges. The concept of trading in "futures" goes back many years to the trade fairs in Europe and the Far East. Traveling merchants who went from fair to fair would agree to bring a buyer some desired item at a specified time in the future.

The first actual organized futures trading started in Japan around 1700, while the first American futures exchange, the Chicago Board of Trade, began operations in 1848. In both cases, it was the erratic supply of grains that prompted development of a futures market solution.

At harvest time, supplies of wheat or corn in the U.S. were plentiful and prices would go down, to the detriment of the producer. A few months later, supplies would dwindle and prices would go up, to the detriment of the miller or other user. Sometimes, there would be too much grain with no buyers at any price; sometimes there would be too little grain with no suppliers at any price.

So sellers and buyers, seeing the need for a more orderly market, began gathering on street corners or in coffee houses and taverns in Chicago, the major Midwest marketing center, to arrange "to arrive" or "forward" contracts for future delivery of grain. While this bargaining practice worked for a number of years, there still were some problems. There always was the danger of defaults. A buyer might back out on his end of an agreement if prices dropped lower than the contract price, for example. There were no uniform quality standards; contract sizes and payment terms were quite variable.

As time passed, traders began meeting in a centralized location and developed formal contract specifications as to size, delivery procedure and quality standards. This evolved into the beginnings of the futures markets as we know them today.

To assure that both parties would live up to their part of the contract, rules at the new exchanges required sellers and buyers to put up security deposits or "margins" — perhaps 10% of the value of the contract — by each party. If either side defaulted, funds then were available to reimburse the innocent party. This margin deposit is not a down payment such as you might make with stocks or with real estate. Rather, this margin should be regarded more as a performance bond to help assure that the contract terms will be fulfilled.

With the arrival of futures markets, famers could sell their crop over an extended period of time. Processors and millers could purchase their supplies in an orderly manner.

With only these two groups in the market, however, it still was difficult for the farmer to find a buyer when he wanted to sell or for a processor to find a seller when he needed to buy. So a third group developed, as speculators discovered they could buy and sell the paper contracts for future delivery, carrying risk for a short period of time in the hopes of making a profit on price changes. These speculators provided the volume of trading that made it possible to get a price quote for wheat or corn at any time. These speculators assumed the risk that farmers (producers) and millers (users) didn't want to assume.

Speculators Play an Important Role

Then, as now, the speculator provides important economic benefits to the market place. Without the futures speculator who wants to trade 1,000 bu. or 5,000 bu. of corn or wheat, the trades among millers and grain merchants would be so few that you would not be able to get a price quote or execute a trade quickly at any time during the day.

But in today's market, thanks to many small speculators, there exists such liquidity that a producer or user of grain can execute a marketing decision within moments of telling his broker what he wants to buy or sell.

In today's futures market, the buyer might be a foreign trading company purchasing soybeans for a nation like Japan. The seller might be a large farmer or a large grain terminal selling grain for several country elevators. The speculators who provide the trading activity so badly needed in the market come from all walks of life. They include homemakers, doctors, construction workers and people from every corner of the economy.

Futures Markets in Action

Here's a real-life example of how futures trading helps businessmen control their financial risk. Note the many transactions which take place. In each transaction, a futures speculator may play an important role. Since you are interested in multiplying your money in the futures market, that speculator could be you.

A soybean farmer whose crop is looking good in August may decide to "lock in" the current price of $6.70 per bu. on Chicago futures for 5,000 bu. of his expected fall crop. To keep this example simple, we will ignore the "basis," or normal price difference between the futures market price and the farmer's local cash market price. Once the farmer decides to sell a 5,000-bu. futures contract, someone must buy a 5,000-bu. contract. If you're bullish on beans, you buy, hoping the price will go higher. A 10¢ price rise increases the value of your contract by $500 for each 5,000 bushels. After the futures market sale, the farmer may decide to hold the futures contract until the day he takes his soybeans to the local elevator. During that period, the farmer is isolated from the impact of a price move, either higher or lower. He is hedged.

Elevator Locks in Inventory Value

When the farmer delivers his soybeans to a local market, he usually buys back, or "offsets," his futures contract on the same day. That requires a seller, most likely a different speculator than the one who originally bought his contract. At that point, the local elevator becomes the owner of the soybeans, which carries a high degree of risk. To eliminate that price risk, the elevator owner may then sell a 5,000-bu. soybean futures contract on the Chicago

Board of Trade. Another speculator or trader is required to take the other side of this transaction.

Processor Locks in Profit Margin

The elevator may later sell its 5,000 bu. of soybeans to a soybean processor like Central Soya, a company in the business of crushing soybeans for the end products of soybean meal and soybean oil. At that point, the elevator lifts its hedge by buying back or "covering" its "short" futures contract which it sold earlier. The processor may sell futures contracts of soybean meal and soybean oil against his purchase of cash soybeans to "lock in" the crushing margin or gross profit. Each of these transactions is greatly facilitated by a speculator interested in taking an opposite position.

Hog Producer Locks in Costs

Back in August when our soybean producer decided to sell a 5,000-bu. contract of soybeans, another farmer — this one specializing in hog production — decided to buy a 100-ton January soybean meal contract. That contract, along with purchases of corn futures contracts, allowed the hog producer to "lock in" most of his production costs.

By late December or early January, the hog farmer might be ready to cover his hedges by selling his meal and corn futures contracts and taking actual delivery of cash meal and corn purchased locally. (Very few farmers or speculators find the need to actually make or take delivery on a futures contract. You will use the futures contract as a tool to accept risk in hopes of making a profit before the delivery date of the contract.)

When the hog producer takes delivery of the soybean meal, the processor lifts his hedge by buying back the meal futures contract he sold earlier.

Hog Producer Locks in Profit

In January, the hog producer might look ahead to June live hog futures and decide he can lock in a good profit at $45 per cwt. So he sells June live hog futures. Now, with both his hog production cost and selling price locked in, the farmer can concentrate on producing the hogs without fear of major price changes suddenly eroding his profits.

Packer Locks in Hog Price

By March, a meat packer may be looking at his orders for the months ahead and find it desirable to lock in the price for his summer hog needs. He then buys hog futures.

Then, in an effort to tie down a profit on a portion of his production, the packer may sell frozen pork bellies (bacon) futures contracts.

By June, the farmer offsets or buys his futures contracts when he delivers the hogs. The packer offsets his futures position by selling the hog futures contracts purchased earlier. Again, each transaction requires a speculator or some other trader to complete the trade.

When the packer sells his bacon to a retail chain store, he then offsets his pork belly position in the futures market. Finally, the bacon makes it to the store shelf but only after at least 17 futures market transactions have helped control the ownership risk.

Speculator Helps Make Trades

In each of the transactions, the commercial man who wanted to place or lift a hedge expected to do it immediately upon placing his order. The farmer who sold the contract of soybeans, for example, didn't want to wait for hours to find out if or when his order was executed. But if the market were limited exclusively to the commercial interest, there would be fewer trades each day and long delays in getting an order filled.

That's where you, as a speculator, play an important role. Because many speculators buy and sell regularly, there is always a "liquid" market. A liquid market is one where there always are ready buyers and sellers. The many small traders provide the liquidity that makes it easy for a farmer, processor or other commercial user to execute a trade within seconds of the time the order is placed.

Even more important, the small speculator helps carry the price risk. By accepting price risk, the speculator helps minimize the ultimate cost of food to the consumer. Whenever there is a large amount of uncontrolled risk, there needs to be a wider profit margin to encourage producers to take the chance. By accepting some of the risk of ownership which producers choose not to carry, the futures speculator assists in the food production process.

Liquidity also is provided by many small speculators. Liquidity may not always be present in a market where there is big volume — volume does not mean liquidity. Two large commercials, one buying 5 million bu. and the other selling 5 million bu., can make a big volume. But that kind of volume doesn't help a producer who wants to sell 5,000 bu. immediately. It is the small speculator who buys and sells in hopes of earning a profit from his risk, who provides the liquid market.

Who are these speculators who perform this valuable service? Certainly, some are professionals — the pit traders who "scalp" the market for small, quick gains; the fund managers; the floor brokers — but most are just normal people who speculate a little as a sideline to some other occupation.

The Typical Futures Trader

A Chicago Mercantile Exchange survey in the fall of 1970 showed a typical futures trader would be a 45-year-old college-educated man who's most likely to be in a white collar profession earning a good, but not exceptional, salary. Most are short-term traders and over half trade only one or two contracts at a time. Hardly anything there describes the speculator as the greedy person that some imagine.

A Commodity Futures Trading Commission study in the summer of 1976 also showed that three out of every five futures accounts had less than $5,000 in equity. Nearly 90% of all futures accounts are smaller than $20,000 — hardly the big-money picture of speculators you sometimes get. That study also indicated there were only 116,000 futures accounts, at all exchanges at that time — nothing like the millions who have securities accounts. Of these 116,000 accounts, more than three-fourths were classified as speculative and only one-fourth as hedging accounts.

Futures trading is not just a game rich folks play with each other. Because people in cash commodity businesses can't afford to carry all the risk themselves, they look for people like you to share the risk of price fluctuation.

Their motivation may be to reduce risk or maximize profits on a commodity they grow or use. Your motivation is to get a good return on your risk capital.

3
Which Commodity Should You Trade

Japanese rice contracts were the first form of futures trading. They were developed in the 1600s. Wealthy landlords collected their rents as a share of their tenants' rice crops. But weather was no more reliable then than now. As a result, the size of the crop varied with the weather. Rents varied with the size of the crop.

But 17th century Japan had a money economy, and landlords had to pay their bills with cash, not rice. To have cash available, landlords shipped rice to regional warehouse points. Then a portion of the crop could be sold whenever they needed money.

To speed up the process of getting cash, landlords began to sell their warehouse receipts — called rice tickets. Merchants began buying the tickets in anticipation of their needs. As futures trading became accepted, more rules developed. Many of the rules are the same as current trading rules of most exchanges. For instance:

1. Life of contracts was limited.
2. Contracts were standardized.
3. Grades for different contract periods were established in advance of trade and were binding.
4. Contracts were not carried over.
5. A clearinghouse was established. All trades were made through the clearinghouse.
6. Each trader had to establish a line of credit with the clearinghouse before he could trade.

Japanese rice contracts had one failing — cash rice could not be delivered to fulfill a futures contract commitment. That made it possible for cash and futures markets to move in opposite directions. Because of the chaos, the government eliminated futures trading in rice. But the ban was short-lived. Soon after futures trading was banned, cash price fluctuations became violent. Within two years, rice futures trading again had government sanction. But this time, physical delivery was allowed. The result was a more predictable relationship between cash and futures. This made the futures contract viable.

First U.S. Futures Market

The Chicago Board of Trade opened on Mar. 13, 1848. The first contract traded was a 3,000-bu. lot of corn. Terms of the contract authorized June delivery of 3,000 bu. of corn at 1¢ discount to the Mar. 13 price.

The first contracts were not formalized; some were only verbal commitments. Such informality did not last long. As soon as speculators began to enter the market, they took on the role of middlemen. That called for formalized exchange rules, most of which were similar to the Japanese rice futures markets of earlier times:

1. Commodities traded on exchanges had to be easily graded.
2. Commodity grading was government supervised.
3. Payment of the futures contract had to be set at time of delivery.
4. Price reporting was made public knowledge.
5. Both buyers and sellers had to establish financial credibility.
6. Trade volume had to be large enough for a viable market.

As trade grew, U.S. exchanges were established near the major trade routes. The New York exchanges specialized in commodities for international export and import trade. The Chicago markets were near major water and rail routes for interior and export grain movement. Chicago was also the major market for livestock, especially cattle, in earlier days.

Trading Today's Futures Markets

Whenever you buy or sell futures contracts, you are entering a legal agreement. The contract is your bond that you will fulfill that legal obligation. The clearinghouse is the court that sorts out the legal obligations. The clearinghouse assumes one side of all the open contracts. If the broker is short, for instance, the clearinghouse is long. If the clearinghouse did not take the opposite position on every trade, then one broker who is short could deal only with the broker who takes the original offsetting position. There would have to be a mutual agreement between the two brokers before the contract would be liquidated.

Legal obligations of futures contracts include the responsibility of the buyer and seller to post a bond. This bond is called initial margin. If the market moves against the trader's position, he must continue to deposit enough bond or margin money to keep his equity at a prescribed amount. The margin protects the broker. The broker's legal rights include the option to offset a client's futures position if his margin is below the brokerage house's prescribed limit.

Exchanges set margin minimums. However, individual brokerage firms may require more margin than the prescribed exchange minimums; they cannot prescribe less. The list of margin requirements on page 48 is typical of most firms. Margin minimums are always subject to change. Consequently, many brokerage firms issue their requirements monthly, along with the client's monthly trade summary.

Initial margin is the amount of money a trader must have in his account before initiating a position. Maintenance margin is the minimum account balance before the trader gets a "margin call." When a trader gets a margin call, he must deposit enough money in the account to bring his equity back to the inital margin. For some commodities, the difference between initial and maintenance margins is very small, so it takes only a small move against the trader's position to produce a margin call.

Margins are lower for spreads than for outright positions. Spread margins in corn, for example, may be only one-fifth the requirement for outright positions because there generally is less risk with spreads. Generally, there is also less potential in corn spreads vs. outright positions on a single contract basis. However, since a trader can establish five spread positions with the same amount of margin money as one outright position, the spread may have equal — or greater — potential. That's especially true in lackluster markets.

Not All Contracts Are Tradeable

While certain futures contracts may fit the needs of producers and users, they don't measure up to the speculator's criteria. The speculator needs more than margin money to consider trading just any commodity. One important factor is the contract's "liquidity," the actual trading activity of a contract as reflected by volume and open interest.

Volume: Daily volume is the number of contracts changing hands during the day's trading hours. In general, the lower the daily volume of trade, the better the chances of an erratic price move. Pork bellies, for instance, do not provide a very liquid market. If you don't believe it, try a market order near the close of the day's session in some back contract. You'll very likely get filled 50 points away from the last price you saw. You're also much more subject to limit moves on news that would move prices of more heavily traded commodities very little.

Most major agricultural commodities have excellent liquidity because of high daily volume. These commodities are day traders' favorites. Market orders placed in these commodities result in acceptable fills in all but the most rapidly moving markets.

The most widely published source of daily volume is the *Wall Street Journal*. Brokerage offices which subscribe to commodity news wires also have daily volume figures.

Open interest: The number of outstanding contracts is open interest. Each contract is counted only once. Because there is a buyer on one side of the contract and a seller on the other, there are actually twice as many market participants as the open interest tally shows.

Many people confuse volume and open interest. The difference between the two is the number of day trades made during the session. Take the example of a lightly-traded contract that has just come on the Board. If today is the first trading day and there are 10 trades made during the session, both volume and open interest tallies would be 10, if all these positions are carried overnight.

But if the 10 trades made during the day are all offset before the session is over, then the total number of trades made during the day grows to 20 — the day's volume. However, if all the trades are offset before the trading session is over, open interest would be zero because no open commitments are carried overnight.

As futures contracts near maturity, open interest usually falls.

That's because most speculators have no interest in making or taking delivery. They offset positions before the contract matures. To do that, longs sell to the shorts before delivery begins. If no offset is made, the longs must be prepared to accept delivery of the contract and ante up the full value of the contract. Shorts who do not buy in to offset earlier sales must make delivery of the actual commodity to an authorized delivery point. Staying in to the end is a game for commercials and locals, not the average speculator. If you want to keep your commitment, the best general rule of thumb is to roll your position forward into a more distant futures contract before first notice day.

In general, speculators should stay out of markets where open interest is less than 5,000 contracts. If you don't trade these "thin" markets carefully, you'll probably get beaten up on fills and may see enough volatility to make you wish you were playing Old Maid. Stops are just not compatible with thin markets.

Risk: Reward Ratio

We've seen lists of futures "beginners should not trade." We're not willing to make such a blanket approach.

Whether you should or should not trade often depends at which stage of the market you enter. For instance, when prices are in the bottom 20% of their 5-year range, you may be more comfortable with that commodity than with a "familiar" commodity in the middle of its 5-year range.

The stage at which you enter a market is as important as the commodity you choose to trade. Not every commodity offers a reasonable opportunity every day.

Commodities Available to Traders

Futures exchanges exist around the world today, offering well over 100 contracts for trade. Futures contracts are as exotic as London gold bullion, Winnipeg flaxseed or the Sydney Future Exchange's greasy wool.

At the end of this chapter is a list of futures traded on exchanges. If you want to trade foreign markets, keep in mind that you may have a tough time finding a corner brokerage house to handle your business. Also note that for some futures you have a choice of several exchanges to trade. The choice of which market you trade should boil down to your broker's preference and your own experience as to which exchange gives you better executions.

Chicago Mercantile Exchange

Live cattle are the star of the show at the Chicago Merc, if open interest is the main indicator of popularity.

Live hogs and pork bellies are also favorites of active speculation. Like the cattle contracts, they are favorites because the meats are trending commodities. Trend-following systems — point-and-figure, moving average, etc. — usually show some of their best profits in these markets. Even the commodity funds find enough volume to allow them to trade hefty quantities of hog and cattle contracts without rippling the market.

Lumber futures on the CME have tended to be a good trending market for technicians to follow.

International Monetary Market of the Chicago Mercantile Exchange

"Just like a soybean bull market all the time," is a comment we've heard echoing through the halls of currency traders. Currencies obey the laws of technical analysis very well. If you trade trendlines, give currencies a look. Currencies and index futures have become the major glamour markets among speculators.

One word of warning about currencies: politics. It's hard to evaluate currency fundamentals when you have to cope with political possibilities, too. Traders who were on the wrong side of the market when the Mexican peso was devalued may not be trading futures any more.

Keep in mind risks associated with trading currencies are always the highest when the market is the most volatile. Volatile markets may force governments to make politically expedient decisions. If you enter currencies during a time of relatively low volatility, you'll cut these kinds of risks dramatically.

IMM currencies (Deutsche mark, British pound, Japanese yen, Canadian dollar, French franc, Swiss franc and Mexican peso) have grown in acceptance generally, although the major currencies understandably enjoy the greater volume.

In addition, the IMM has created the interest rate futures of Treasury Bills (3 months), Eurodollar (3-month time deposit) and Domestic Bank Certificates of Deposit ($1,000,000).

To complete the list, there are two stock index futures which differ only in size: The S&P 500 Stock Index and the S&P 100, the former being the index value in dollars times 500 while the latter is (obviously) multiplied by 100.

In addition, the IMM has provided options on the Deutsche mark and S&P 500 futures.

Chicago Board of Trade

For many years, the grains led all commodities in trading activity. That was because of heavy commercial trade volume.

But grains sometimes give trend-followers soul-searching fits. Prices often tend to work erractically higher, many times violating trendlines as they go. However, an understanding of bar charts will serve you as well in grains as in most other commodities. Corn often drops like a stone from its spring-summer highs into its normal harvest-time lows. An understanding of seasonal patterns and government loan and reserve relationships is an aid in achieving success. Spread trades in corn also are prone to predictably profitable seasonal patterns.

Nearly everything that can be said about corn also goes for oats. Oats are less volatile and, consequently, require less trading margin than corn. They're a good choice in small portfolios. But if you use stops and market orders, keep them in the lead contract or you won't like the looks of your confirmation slips.

Wheat's moves tend to be larger than those of either corn or oats. Wheat also trends better, systems fans should note. Characteristic price movement is in broad "V" formations.

Traders who like action gravitate towards soybeans. Any experienced trader who uses a trend-following system probably will tell you the soybean complex is among his favorite commodities. That's because of the complex's tendency for long moves. Highs and lows for the year often range several dollars around the average price. Once the action gets underway, it often has freight-train-like momentum, even though there often are violent bear market rallies and equally violent bull market dips. The trademarks of the soybean complex are V-bottoms and V-tops.

Position holders who protect their losses with stops usually will find meal and oil less erratic and less prone to "picking stops." That's because beans are the day trader's favorite commodity, which tends to exaggerate interday fluctuations. But the products are dominated by commercial, not speculator, activity. That's why the products tend to be less volatile. Also, a single contract of meal and another of oil usually require no more margin than a contract for 5,000 bu. of beans.

Oil is a favorite of bar chart traders. It obeys trendlines very well. Here's a very important fact on the bean complex: The products often tend to move separately. A strong bull move in meal, for instance, often precedes a strong bull move in oil. The lead time may be a couple of months or more.

The financial futures traded at the Chicago Board of Trade have now grown to include T-Bonds, GNMA's, T-Notes (10 years) and the MMI, or Major Market Stock Index. Also traded are the 1,000-oz. silver contract, one kilo gold, Western plywood, and crude petroleum. The last three are only moderately active. ·

The Chicago Board of Trade has instituted options on the T-Bond futures.

Commodity Exchange (Comex)

New York's Comex is known as a metals market, although it does have several interest rate contracts. Copper, gold, silver and aluminum are the metals contracts traded. Comex does take close-only stops. That may be considered an advantage by some traders of the volatile precious metals.

Other New York Exchanges

Three other commodity exchanges are located at the Commodities Exchange Center in the World Trade Center along with Comex: New York Mercantile Exchange, New York Cotton Exchange and the Coffee, Sugar & Cocoa Exchange. In addition, there is the New York Futures Exchange, which trades financial futures.

Many of the contracts on these exchanges aren't "tradeable" by our standards of a 5,000-contract open interest minimum. Some of the contracts are popular with funds and foreign traders. You may see rather large price movements out of congestion areas as these larger traders enter a rather thin market.

The NYCE's cotton contract has always been a high flier in popularity terms. We'd recommend it to any technical systems trader. It corresponds especially well to time and price cycle analysis. Orange juice trading has gained in popularity since freezes have made prices especially volatile. One thing we've noted about the juice contract — it often tends to move in the direction opposite to the overall direction of the commodity complex.

Kansas City Board of Trade

KCBT wheat is the hard, red winter variety. CBT wheat is soft red winter. KCBT open interest usually is less than half of that for CBT wheat. Prices tend to move in tandem, but many of the trading opportunities are arbitrage possibilities vs. the Chicago and Minneapolis wheat markets. KCBT's milo contract is not active currently. The Kansas City Board of Trade instituted a stock index future. It is known as the Value Line Average Index. Other than that, their trade is limited to wheat.

MidAmerica Commodity Exchange

MidAm offers almost everything you always wanted to trade on the CBT or CME but couldn't afford. MidAm's mini-contracts are great for aspiring speculators who've advanced from the paper trading stage and want to get their feet wet. We advise beginning traders to diversify. The way to do that realistically with an account under $5,000 is to go with the minis.

Minneapolis Grain Exchange

MGE wheat contracts represent some arbitrage opportunities with KCBT and CBT contracts. Otherwise, we'd consider it a market for producers and users, not speculators. The Minneapolis Grain Exchange trades spring wheat futures, although they have tried to initiate other futures, particularly sunflower seed.

Winnipeg Commodity Exchange

In addition to the grains and oilseeds Winnipeg has a small market in gold and silver and they are undoubtedly trying to expand their horizons.

Futures Contracts

Commodity	Trading months	Trading hours (local time)	Contract size	Minimum price fluctuation	Daily limit

Chicago Board of Trade

Commodity	Trading months	Trading hours (local time)	Contract size	Minimum price fluctuation	Daily limit
Corn	Mar/May/July Sept/Dec	9:30-1:15	5,000 bu.	1/4¢/bu. = $12.50	10¢/bu. = $500
Oats	Mar/May/July Sept/Dec	9:30-1:15	5,000 bu.	1/4¢/bu. = $12.50	6¢/bu. = $300
Soybeans	Jan/Mar/May/July Aug/Sept/Nov	9:30-1:15	5,000 bu.	1/4¢/bu. = $12.50	30¢/bu. = $1,500
Soybean Meal	Jan/Mar/May/July Aug/Sept/Oct/Dec	9:30-1:15	100 tons	10¢/ton = $10	$10/ton = $1,000
Soybean Oil	Jan/Mar/May/July Aug/Sept/Oct/Dec	9:30-1:15	60,000 lb.	1/100¢/lb. = $6	1¢/lb. = $600
Wheat	Mar/May/July Sept/Dec	9:30-1:15	5,000 bu.	1/4¢/bu. = $12.50	20¢/bu. = $1,000
Crude Oil	Feb/June/July/Aug Sept/Oct/Dec	8:30-2:10	1,000 barrels (42,000 gal.)	1¢/barrel = $10	$1/barrel = $1,000
GNMA CDR	Mar/June Sept/Dec	8:00-2:00	$100,000 principal	1/32 pt. = $31.25	64/32 pt. = $2,000
U.S. Treasury Bonds	Mar/June Sept/Dec	8:00-2:00	$100,000 8% coupon	1/32 pt. = $31.25	64/32 pt. = $2,000
U.S. Treasury Notes (6½-10 yr.)	Mar/June Sept/Dec	8:00-2:00	$100,000 8% coupon	1/32 pt. = $31.25	64/32 pt. = $2,000
GNMA II	Mar/June Sept/Dec	8:00-2:00	$100,000 principal	1/32 pt. = $31.25	64/32 pt. = $2,000
Long-term Municipal Bond Index	Mar/June Sept/Dec	8:00-2:00	$1,000 × Bond Buyer Municipal Bond Index	1/32 pt. = $31.25	64/32 pt. = $2,000
30-Day Repurchase Agreements	Mar/June Sept/Dec	8:00-2:00	$2,500,000	1/100 pt. = $20.83	1 pt. = $2,083

Commodity	Trading months	Trading hours (local time)	Contract size	Minimum price fluctuation	Daily limit
90-Day Repurchase Agreements	Mar/June Sept/Dec	8:00-2:00	$1,000,000	1/100 pt. = $25	1 pt. = $2,500
Commodity Index	Mar/June Sept/Dec	Not determined	$500 × Commodity Index	1/40 = $12.50	None
Major Market Index	March cycle and consecutive months	8:45-3:15	$100 × Major Market Index*	1/8 = $12.50	None
AMEX Market Value Index	March cycle and consecutive months	8:45-3:15	$100 × Market Value Index*	1/8 = $12.50	None
Gold	Feb/Apr/June Aug/Oct/Dec	8:00-1:30	1 kilogram = 32.15 oz.	10¢/oz. = $3.22	$50/oz. = $1,607.50
Silver	Feb/Mar/Apr June/Aug/Oct/Dec	8:05-1:25	1,000 troy oz.	1/10¢/oz. = $5	50¢/oz. = $500
Western Plywood	Jan/Mar/May July/Sept/Nov	9:00-1:05	76,032 sq. ft.	10¢/1,000 sq. ft. = $7.60	$7/1,000 sq. ft. = $532

*Under review.

Chicago Mercantile Exchange

Commodity	Trading months	Trading hours (local time)	Contract size	Minimum price fluctuation	Daily limit
Broilers, Fresh	Feb/Apr/June/July Aug/Oct/Dec	9:10-1:00	30,000 lb.	2.5/100¢/lb. = $7.50	2¢/lb. = $600
Cattle, Feeder	Jan/Mar/Apr/May Aug/Sept/Oct/Nov	9:05-12:45	44,000 lb.	2.5/100¢/lb. = $11	1.5¢/lb. = $660
Cattle, Live	Feb/Apr/June Aug/Oct/Dec	9:05-12:45	40,000 lb.	2.5/100¢/lb. = $10	1.5¢/lb. = $600
Eggs, Fresh White	All months except August	9:20-1:00	22,500 doz.	5/100¢/doz. = $11.25	2¢/doz. = $450
Hogs, Live	Feb/Apr/June/July Aug/Oct/Dec	9:10-1:00	30,000 lb.	2.5/100¢/lb. = $7.50	1.5¢/lb. = $450
Pork Bellies	Feb/Mar/May July/Aug	9:10-1:00	38,000 lb.	2.5/100¢/lb. = $9.50	2¢/lb. = $760

Commodity	Trading months	Trading hours (local time)	Contract size	Minimum price fluctuation	Daily limit

International Monetary Market of the Chicago Mercantile Exchange

Commodity	Trading months	Trading hours (local time)	Contract size	Minimum price fluctuation	Daily limit
Deutsche Mark	Jan/Mar/Apr/June July/Sept/Oct/Dec and spot month	7:30-1:20	125,000 DM	$0.0001/DM = $12.50	$0.01 = $1,250
Canadian Dollar	Jan/Mar/Apr/June July/Sept/Oct/Dec and spot month	7:30-1:26	100,000 CD	$0.0001/CD = $10	$0.0075 = $750
French Franc	Jan/Mar/Apr/June July/Sept/Oct/Dec and spot month	7:30-1:28	250,000 FF	$0.00005/FF = $12.50	$0.005 = $1,250
Swiss Franc	Jan/Mar/Apr/June July/Sept/Oct/Dec and spot month	7:30-1:16	125,000 SF	$0.0001/SF = $12.50	$0.0150 = $1,875
British Pound	Jan/Mar/Apr/June July/Sept/Oct/Dec and spot month	7:30-1:24	25,000 BP	$0.0005/BP = $12.50	$0.05 = $1,250
Mexican Peso	Jan/Mar/Apr/June July/Sept/Oct/Dec and spot month	7:30-1:18	1,000,000 MP	$0.00001/MP = $10	$0.00150 = $1,500
Japanese Yen	Jan/Mar/Apr/June July/Sept/Oct/Dec and spot month	7:30-1:22	12,500,000 JY	$0.000001/JY = $12.50	$0.0001 = $1,250
Gold	Jan/Mar/Apr/June July/Sept/Oct/Dec and spot month	8:00-1:30	100 troy oz.	10¢/oz. = $10	$50/oz. = $5,000
Treasury Bills (90-day)	Mar/June Sept/Dec	8:00-2:00	$1,000,000	1 pt. = $25	60 pt. = $1,500
Domestic Certificates of Deposit (3-month)	Mar/June Sept/Dec	7:30-2:00	$1,000,000	1 pt. = $25	80 pt. = $2,000
Eurodollar Time Deposit (3-month)	Mar/June/Sept/Dec and spot month	7:30-2:00	$1,000,000	1 pt. = $25	100 pt. = $2,500

Commodity	Trading months	Trading hours (local time)	Contract size	Minimum price fluctuation	Daily limit

Index and Option Market
of the Chicago Mercantile Exchange

Commodity	Trading months	Trading hours (local time)	Contract size	Minimum price fluctuation	Daily limit
Standard & Poor's 500 Stock Index	Mar/June Sept/Dec	9:00-3:15	500 × S&P Stock Index	5 pt. = $25	None
Standard & Poor's 100 Stock Index	Next four months and Mar/June Sept/Dec	9:00-3:15	200 × S&P 100 Stock Index	5 pt. = $10	None
No. 2 Fuel Oil	Every calendar month	8:30-2:30	1,000 barrels (42,000 gal.)	0.025¢ = $10.50	3¢/gal. = $1,260
Leaded Regular Gasoline	Every calendar month	8:30-2:30	1,000 barrels (42,000 gal.)	0.025¢ = $10.50	3¢/gal. = $1,260
Lumber (random-length)	Jan/Mar/May July/Sept/Nov	9:00-1:05	130,000 bd. ft.	10¢/1,000 bd. ft. = $13	$5/1,000 bd. ft. = $650

Chicago Rice and Cotton Exchange
(Formerly New Orleans Commodity Exchange; now trades on floor of MidAmerica Commodity Exchange)

Commodity	Trading months	Trading hours (local time)	Contract size	Minimum price fluctuation	Daily limit
Rough Rice	Jan/Mar/May July/Sept/Nov	8:45-1:45	2,000 cwt. (200,000 lb.)	1¢/cwt. = $20	30¢/cwt. = $600

Coffee, Sugar & Cocoa Exchange Inc.

Commodity	Trading months	Trading hours (local time)	Contract size	Minimum price fluctuation	Daily limit
Cocoa	Mar/May/July Sept/Dec	9:30-3:00	10 metric tons	$1/metric ton = $10	$88/metric ton = $880
Coffee "C"	Mar/May/July Sept/Dec	9:45-2:30	37,500 lb.	1/100¢/lb. = $3.75	4¢/lb. = $1,500
Sugar No. 11 (world)	Jan/Mar/May July/Sept/Oct	10:00-1:45	112,000 lb.	1/100¢/lb. = $11.20	1/2¢/lb. = $560
Sugar No. 12 (domestic)	Jan/Mar/May July/Sept/Nov	10:00-1:45	112,000 lb.	1/100¢/lb. = $11.20	1/2¢/lb. = $560

Commodity	Trading months	Trading hours (local time)	Contract size	Minimum price fluctuation	Daily limit

Commodity Exchange Inc. (COMEX)

Commodity	Trading months	Trading hours (local time)	Contract size	Minimum price fluctuation	Daily limit
Aluminum	Current calendar month, next two months and Jan/Mar/May July/Sept/Dec	9:30-2:15	40,000 lb.	0.05¢/lb. = $20	5¢/lb. = $2,000
Copper	"	9:50-2:00	25,000 lb.	5/100¢/lb. = $12.50	5¢/lb. = $1,250
Silver	"	9:05-2:25	5,000 troy oz.	10/100¢/oz. = $5	50¢/oz. = $2,500
Gold	Current calendar month, next two months and Feb/Apr/June Aug/Oct/Dec	9:00-2:30	100 troy oz.	10¢/oz. = $10	$25/oz. = $2,500

Kansas City Board of Trade

Commodity	Trading months	Trading hours (local time)	Contract size	Minimum price fluctuation	Daily limit
Wheat (hard red winter)	Mar/May/July Sept/Dec	9:30-1:15	5,000 bu.	1/4¢/bu. = $12.50	25¢/bu. = $1,250
Value Line Stock Index	Mar/June Sept/Dec	9:00-3:15	500 times the futures price	0.05 = $25	None
Mini Value Line Stock Index	Mar/June Sept/Dec	9:00-3:15	100 times the futures price	0.05 = $5	None

MidAmerica Commodity Exchange

Commodity	Trading months	Trading hours (local time)	Contract size	Minimum price fluctuation	Daily limit
Cattle, Live	Feb/Apr/June Aug/Oct/Dec	9:05-1:00	20,000 lb.	2.5/100¢/lb. = $5	1.5¢/lb. = $300
Hogs, Live	Feb/Apr/June July/Aug/Oct/Dec	9:10-1:15	15,000 lb.	2.5/100¢/lb. = $3.75	1.5¢/lb. = $225
Corn	Mar/May/July Sept/Dec	9:30-1:30	1,000 bu.	1/8¢/bu. = $1.25	10¢/bu. = $100
Oats	Mar/May/July Sept/Dec	9:30-1:30	1,000 bu.	1/8¢/bu. = $10	6¢/bu. = $60
Soybeans	Jan/Mar/May July/Aug/Sept/Nov	9:30-1:30	1,000 bu.	1/8¢/bu. = $1.25	30¢/bu. = $300

Commodity	Trading months	Trading hours (local time)	Contract size	Minimum price fluctuation	Daily limit
Wheat	Mar/May/July Sept/Dec	9:30-1:30	1,000 bu.	1/8¢/bu. = $1.25	20¢/bu. = $200
Gold	Mar/June/Sept Dec	8:00-1:40	33.2 fine troy oz.	10¢/oz. = $3.32	$50/oz. = $1,660
Silver (Chicago contract)	Current month and any subsequent months, up to 12-15 months ahead	8:05-1:40	1,000 troy oz.	10/100¢/oz. = $1	50¢/oz. = $500
Silver (New York contract)	Same as above for Chicago contract				
U.S. Treasury Bonds	Mar/June Sept/Dec	8:00-2:15	$50,000 face value	1/32 pt. = $15.62	64/32 pt. = $1,000
U.S. Treasury Bills (90-day)	Mar/June Sept/Dec	8:00-2:15	$500,000 face value	1/10 pt. = $12.50	60 pt. = $750
Sugar (domestic refined)	Jan/Mar/May July/Sept/Nov	9:00-1:00	40,000 lb.	1/100¢/lb. = $4	1/2¢/lb. = $200
British Pound	Mar/June Sept/Dec	7:30-1:34	12,500 BP	$0.0005/BP = $6.25	$0.05/BP = $625
Canadian Dollar	Mar/June Sept/Dec	7:30-1:36	50,000 CD	$0.0001/ CD = $5	$0.0075/ CD = $375
Deutsche Mark	Mar/June Sept/Dec	7:30-1:30	62,500 DM	$0.0001/DM = $6.25	$0.01/DM = $625
Japanese Yen	Mar/June Sept/Dec	7:30-1:32	6,250,000 JY	$0.000001/ JY = $6.25	$0.0001/JY = $625
Swiss Franc	Mar/June Sept/Dec	7:30-1:26	62,000 SF	$0.0001/SF = $6.25	$0.015/SF = $937

Minneapolis Grain Exchange

Commodity	Trading months	Trading hours (local time)	Contract size	Minimum price fluctuation	Daily limit
Spring Wheat	Mar/May/July Sept/Dec	9:30-1:15	5,000 bu.	1/8¢/bu. = $6.25	20¢/bu. = $1,000
Sunflower Seeds	Jan/Mar/May July/Nov	9:25-1:20	100,000 lb.	1/100¢/lb. = $10	1/2¢/lb. = $500

Commodity	Trading months	Contract size	Minimum price fluctuation	Trading hours (local time)

New York Cotton Exchange

Cotton No. 2	Mar/May/July Oct/Dec	10:30-3:00	50,000 lb. (approx. 100 bales)	1/100¢/lb. = $5	2¢/lb. = $1,000
Orange Juice	Jan/Mar/May July/Sept/Nov	10:15-2:45	15,000 lb.	5/100¢/lb. = $7.50	5¢/lb. = $750
Propane Gas (liquified)	All months	10:45-3:15	1,000 barrels (42,000 gal.)	1/100¢/gal. = $4.20	2¢/gal. = $840

New York Futures Exchange

NYSE Composite Stock Index	Mar/June Sept/Dec	10:00-4:15	500 × index	5 pt. = $25	None

New York Mercantile Exchange

Palladium	All months	9:00-2:20	100 troy oz.	5¢/oz. = $5	$6/oz. = $600
Platinum	All months	9:10-2:30	50 troy oz.	10¢/oz. = $5	$20/oz. = $1,000
Potatoes	Mar/Apr May/Nov	9:45-2:00	100,000 lb.	1¢/50 lb. = $20	40¢/50 lb. = $800
No. 2 Heating Oil (New York)	All months	10:00-3:05	42,000 gal.	1/100¢/gal. = $4.20	2¢/gal. = $840
Leaded Gasoline	All months	9:45-3:00	42,000 gal.	1/100¢/gal. = $4.20	2¢/gal. = $840
Crude Oil (light sweet)	All months	9:30-3:10	1,000 barrels (42,000 gal.)	1¢/barrel = $10	$1/barrel = $1,000

The Montreal Exchange Mercantile Division

Eastern Lumber	Jan/Mar/May July/Sept/Nov	9:00-3:00	130,000 bd. ft.	U.S. 10¢/ 1,000 bd. ft. = $13	U.S. $5/ 1,000 bd. ft. = $650

Commodity	Trading months	Contract size	Minimum price fluctuation	Trading hours (local time)	

Toronto Futures Exchange

Commodity	Trading months	Contract size	Minimum price fluctuation	Trading hours (local time)	
Canadian Bonds (18-year)	Mar/June Sept/Dec	9:00-3:15	CD $100,000	1/32 pt. = $31.25	2 pt. = $2,000
Canadian T-Bills (13-week)	Mar/June Sept/Dec	9:00-3:15	CD $1,000,000	0.005 pt. = $50	0.150 pt. = $1,500
Toronto Stock Exchange (TSE) 300 Index	Mar/June Sept/Dec	10:00-4:15	10 × index	1 pt. = $10	150 pt. = $1,500
U.S. Dollar	Mar/June Sept/Dec	8:30-3:30	U.S. $100,000	0.01¢ = $10	1¢ = $1,000

The Winnipeg Commodity Exchange

Commodity	Trading months	Contract size	Minimum price fluctuation	Trading hours (local time)	
Domestic Feed Barley	Mar/May/July Oct/Dec	9:30-1:15	100 metric tons	10¢/ton = $10	$5/ton = $500
Alberta Domestic Feed Barley	Feb/Apr/June Sept/Nov	9:30-1:15	20 metric tons	10¢/ton = $2	$5/ton = $100
Flaxseed	Mar/May/July Oct/Dec	9:30-1:15	100 metric tons	10¢/ton = $10	$10/ton = $1,000
Domestic Feed Oats	Mar/May/July Oct/Dec	9:30-1:15	100 metric tons	10¢/ton = $10	$5/ton = $500
Rapeseed	Jan/Mar/June Sept/Nov	9:30-1:15	100 metric tons	10¢/ton = $10	$10/ton = $1,000
Rye	Mar/May/July Oct/Dec	9:30-1:15	100 metric tons	10¢/ton = $10	$5/ton = $500
Domestic Feed Wheat	Mar/May/July Oct/Dec	9:30-1:15	100 metric tons	10¢/ton = $10	$5/ton = $500
Gold	Mar/June/Sept Dec	8:25-1:30	20 oz.	10¢/oz.	$25/oz.
Silver	Jan/Apr/July Oct	8:30-1:35	200 oz.	1¢/oz. = $2	50¢/oz. = $100

Commodity	Trading months	Contract size	Minimum price fluctuation	Trading hours (local time)	
Treasury Bills (13-week)	Mar/June/Sept Dec	8:20-1:25	$200,000	One index point	Sixty index points
Long-Term Bonds	Mar/June/Sept Dec	8:20-1:25	$20,000	1/32 of $1 per $100 face value	64/32 of $1 per $100 face value

Overseas Exchanges

The London Commodity Exchange Co. Ltd.

Following are terminal marketing associations represented on the London Commodity Exchange:

London Cocoa Terminal Market Association Ltd.

Cocoa	Mar/May/July Sept/Dec	10 metric tons	1 stg./ton	10:00-5:00; Calls: 10:00, 12:58, 2:30, 3:30, 4:45

Coffee Terminal Market Association of London Ltd.

Coffee (robusta)	Jan/Mar/May July/Sept/Nov	5 metric tons	£1/ton	10:30-5:00; Calls: 10:30, 12:20, 2:45, 4:50

London Rubber Terminal Association Ltd.

Rubber No. 1A	3-month contracts: Jan/Feb/Mar Apr/May/June July/Aug/Sept Oct/Nov/Dec	15 metric tons	£0.10/ton	Calls: 9:45 12:45 (kerb), 2:30, 3:15, 4:30

London Vegetable Oil Terminal Market Association Ltd.

Soybean Oil	Feb/Apr/June Aug/Oct/Dec	25 metric tons	$0.50/ton	Kerb calls: 10:15, 12:15, 2:30, 3:00

(Trading currently suspended)

Commodity	Trading months	Contract size	Minimum price fluctuation	Trading hours (local time)

United Terminal Sugar Market Association Ltd. (London)

Sugar No. 6	Mar/May Aug/Oct/Dec	50 metric tons	$0.20/ton	10:30-4:45; Calls: 10:30, 12:30, 4:45
White Sugar	Feb/Apr/July Sept/Nov Mar/May Aug/Oct/Dec	50 metric tons	$0.20/ton	10:10-4:30; Calls: 10:10, 12:15, 4:30

London and New Zealand Futures Association Ltd.

New Zealand Crossbred Wool	Jan/Mar/May Aug/Oct/Dec	2,500 kilos	N.Z. 1¢/kilo = $25	2:45-3:45

International Petroleum Exchange of London Ltd.

Gas Oil (Equivalent to NYMEX No. 2 heating oil)	Nine consecutive months including current month	100 metric tons	U.S. 25¢/ton = $25	9:30-12:30, 2:45-5:20
Crude Oil	Current month and next six months	1,000 barrels (42,000 gal.)	U.S. 1¢/barrel = $10	9:45-12:05, 2:30-5:20

The GAFTA Soya Bean Meal Futures Association Ltd.

Soybean Meal	Feb/Apr/June/Aug Oct/Dec/Feb	100 metric tons	10 pence/ton	10:30-12:00, 2:45-4:45

Grain & Feed Trade Association Ltd. (London)

EEC Wheat	Jan/Mar/May July/Sept/Nov	100 metric tons	5 pence/ton	11:00-12:30, 2:45-4:00
EEC Barley	Jan/Mar/May Sept/Nov	100 metric tons	5 pence/ton	11:00-12:30, 2:45-4:00

Commodity	Trading months	Contract size	Minimum price fluctuation	Trading hours (local time)

The London Potato Futures Association Ltd.

Potatoes	Nov/Feb/Apr May/Nov	40 metric tons	10 pence/ton	11:00-12:30, 2:45-4:00

London Metal Exchange

Aluminum	(Any single market day between current day—spot—and 3 months forward)	25 metric tons	50 pence/ton	11:55-12:00, 12:55-1:00*, 3:40-3:45, 4:25-4:30
Copper (higher grade)	"	25 metric tons	50 pence/ton	12:00-12:05, 12:30-12:35*, 3:30-3:35, 4:10-4:15
Copper (standard cathodes)	"	25 metric tons	50 pence/ton	12:00-12:05, 12:35-12:40*, 3:30-3:35, 4:15-4:20
Lead	"	25 metric tons	25 pence/ton	12:10-12:15, 12:45-12:50*, 3:20-3:25, 4:00-4:05
Nickel	"	6 metric tons	£1.00/ton	12:20-12:25, 1:00-1:05*, 3:45-3:50, 4:30-4:35
Silver	"	10,000 troy oz.	1/10 pence/oz.	11:50-11:55, 1:05-1:10*, 3:50-3:55, 4:35-4:40
Silver	"	2,000 troy oz.	1/10 pence/oz.	11:50-11:55, 1:05-1:10*, 3:50-3:55, 4:35-4:40
Tin	"	5 metric tons	£1/ton	12:05-12:10, 12:40-12:45*, 3:35-3:40, 4:20-4:25
Zinc	"	25 metric tons	25 pence/ton	12:15-12:20, 12:50-12:55*, 3:25-3:30, 4:10-4:15

*Sessions that yield exchange's official daily prices.

Commodity	Trading months	Contract size	Minimum price fluctuation	Trading hours (local time)

London Gold Futures Market Ltd.

Gold	Current month and next six consecutive months	100 troy oz.	U.S. 10¢/oz. = $10	9:30-12:10 call* 2:00-4:40 call* *Start of closing call, which lasts indefinitely

London Bullion Market

Gold	Spot and forward positions dated	400 troy oz.	None	9:00-4:00 with official spot fixings at 10:30 and 3:00
Silver	Spot and forward positions dated	5,000 fine oz.	1/10 pence/oz.	9:00-4:00 with official fixing at 12:00

The London International Financial Futures Exchange Ltd.

20-Year U.K. Gilt Interest Rate (government stock)	Mar/June Sept/Dec	£50,000 nominal value	£1/32 per £100 nominal = £15.625	9:30-4:15
Three-Month Eurodollar Interest Rate	Mar/June Sept/Dec	U.S. $1,000,000	1 pt. (0.01%) = U.S. $25	8:30-4:00
Three-Month Sterling Interest Rate	Mar/June Sept/Dec	£250,000 (Becomes £500,000 with March 1985 contract)	1 pt. (0.01%) = £6.25	8:20-4:02
British Pound	Mar/June Sept/Dec	£25,000	0.01¢/£ = U.S. $2.50	8:32-4:02
Deutsche Mark	Mar/June Sept/Dec	DM125,000	0.01¢/DM = U.S. $12.50	8:34-4:04
Swiss Franc	Mar/June Sept/Dec	SF125,000	0.01¢/SF = U.S. $12.50	8:36-4:06
Japanese Yen	Mar/June Sept/Dec	JY12,500,000	0.01¢/100 JY = U.S. $12.50	8:30-4:00

Commodity	Trading months	Contract size	Minimum price fluctuation	Trading hours (local time)
U.S. Treasury Bonds	Mar/June Sept/Dec	$100,000 8% coupon	1/32 pt. = $31.25	8:15-3:00
Financial Times Stock Exchange 100 Index	Mar/June Sept/Dec	25 × index	0.05 pt. = £12.50	9:35-3:30

Hong Kong Commodity Exchange Ltd.

Commodity	Trading months	Contract size	Minimum price fluctuation	Trading hours (local time)
Sugar	Jan/Mar/May July/Sept/Oct	112,000 lb.	1/100¢/lb. = $11.20	10:30-12:00, 2:25-4:00
Soybeans	Six consecutive months ahead	66,000 lb.	HK 20¢/bag = HK $100	9:50, 10:50, 12:50, 2:50
Gold	3 months ahead and Feb/Apr/June Aug/Oct/Dec	100 troy oz.	U.S. 10¢/troy oz. = U.S. $10	9:00-12:00, 2:30-5:30

The International Futures Exchange (Bermuda) Ltd. (INTEX)

(Scheduled to open soon)

Commodity	Trading months	Contract size	Minimum price fluctuation	Trading hours (local time)
Gold	Feb/Apr/June Aug/Oct/Dec	100 troy oz.	10¢/oz. = $10	9:30-5:00 initially
Long-Term U.S. Treasury Bond	Mar/June Sept/Dec	$100,000, 8% coupon	1/32 pt. = $31.25	9:45-5:30 initially
Silver	Jan/Mar/May July/Sept/Dec	5,000 troy oz.	$0.001/oz. = $5	9:45-5:15
Ocean Freight Rate Index	Jan/Apr July/Oct	$500 × Drybulk Index	0.05 pt. = $25	9:30-5:30

The Kuala Lumpur Commodity Exchange

Commodity	Trading months	Contract size	Minimum price fluctuation	Trading hours (local time)
Palm Oil	Next six months plus alternate months thereafter	25 metric tons	Malaysian $1/ton = M $25	11:00-12:30, 3:30-6:00

Commodity	Trading months	Contract size	Minimum price fluctuation	Trading hours (local time)
Rubber	Nearby single delivery months and distant delivery quarters up to 15 forward months	25 metric tons for single delivery months, 75 metric tons for delivery quarters	Malaysian 0.25¢/kilogram	10:00-1:00, 4:00-6:30

Paris Commodity Exchange

Commodity	Trading months	Contract size	Minimum price fluctuation	Trading hours (local time)
White Sugar	Mar/May/Aug Oct/Dec	50 metric tons	1.00FF/ton	10:00-1:00, 3:00-7:00
Cocoa	Mar/May/July Sept/Dec	10 metric tons	0.50FF/100 kg	10:30-1:00, 3:00-6:30
Coffee (robusta)	Jan/Mar/May July/Sept/Nov	10 metric tons (and 5 metric tons after July 1984)	1.00FF/100 kg	10:15-1:00, 3:00-6:30
Soybean Meal	Jan/Mar/May/July Sept/Oct/Dec	50 metric tons	0.25FF/100 kg	11:00-1:00, 3:00-6:30

Bolsa de Mercadorias de Sao Paulo

Commodity	Trading months	Contract size	Minimum price fluctuation	Trading hours (local time)
Cotton	Mar/May/July Oct/Dec	500 50-kilo bags	Cr$ 10/15 kilo	10:00-12:00
Coffee	Mar/May/July Sept/Dec	100 60-kilo bags	Cr$ 50/60 kilo	10:20-12:15, 2:15-3:30
Soya Grain	Jan/Mar/May July/Sept/Nov	30 metric tons	Cr$ 10/ton	12:30-4:15
Soya Feed	Jan/Mar/May July/Sept/Nov	25 metric tons	Cr$ 10/ton	11:00-11:40
Soya Oil	Jan/Mar/May July/Sept/Nov	12 metric tons	Cr$ 10/ton	9:50-10:45
Gold	Feb/Apr/June Aug/Oct/Dec	250 grams 1,000 grams	Cr$ 10/gram	11:30-3:40
Corn	Jan/Mar/May July/Sept/Nov	60 metric tons	Cr$ 10/ton	9:30-11:30

Commodity	Trading months	Contract size	Minimum price fluctuation	Trading hours (local time)

Sydney Futures Exchange Ltd.

Commodity	Trading months	Contract size	Minimum price fluctuation	Trading hours (local time)
Cattle, Live (trade steers)	All months	10,000 kilos	1/10 cent/kilo	10:30-12:30, 2:00-4:00
Wool (greasy)	Mar/May/July Oct/Dec	1,500 kilos	1/10 cent/kilo	10:30-12:30, 2:00-4:00
Gold	Mar/June Sept/Dec	50 troy oz.	10¢/oz. = $5	10:30-12:30, 2:00-4:00
Silver	Mar/June Sept/Dec	1,000 troy oz.	1¢/oz. = $10	10:30-12:30, 2:00-4:00
90-Day Bank Accepted Bills of Exchange	Spot month, next 6 mo.; Mar/June Sept/Dec up to 24 mo. out	Aust. $500,000 face value	1 pt. (0.01%)	9:25-12:30, 2:00-4:00
U.S. Dollar	Spot month, next 5 mo.; Mar/June Sept/Dec up to 18 mo. out	U.S. $100,000	A$0.0001/ U.S. $1.00	9:45-12:30, 2:00-4:00
All Ordinaries Share Price Index	Mar/June Sept/Dec	All ordinaries share price index × A$100 (about $50,000)	1 pt.	10:00-12:30, 2:00-3:45
Two-Year Treasury Bond	Mar/June Sept/Dec	Australian $200,000	1 pt. (0.005%)	9:25-12:30, 2:00-3:30

Options on Futures

Options on futures have the same contract months, trading hours, limits, etc., as their underlying futures contracts. This list does not include all those options that may be *included in the agricultural options program scheduled to begin in the fall of 1984. Some exchanges had not made a final determination on contracts by our deadline date.*

Underlying futures contract	Contract size	Strike price increments	Minimum fluctuation	Expiration date
Chicago Board of Trade				
U.S. Treasury Bonds	$100,000	2 pt.	1/64 pt. = $15.62 (1.0 = $1,000)	Noon on Friday at least five business days before first notice day
GNMA II	$100,000 principal	2 pt.	1/64 pt. = $15.625 (1.0 = $1,000)	Second Friday preceding last day of trading in underlying futures
Soybeans	5,000 bu.	25¢ under $8; 50¢ above $8	1/8¢/bu. = $6.25 (1.0 = $50)	Saturday following last trading day
Index and Option Market of the Chicago Mercantile Exchange				
S&P 500 Stock Index	500 × S&P Index	5 pt.	0.05 pt. = $25 (1.0 = $500)	Third Thursday of contract month
Deutsche Mark	125,000 DM	1¢	0.01¢/DM = $12.50 (1.0 = $1,250)	
Coffee, Sugar and Cocoa Exchange				
Sugar No. 11	112,000 lb. (50 long tons)	Varies*	1/100¢/lb. = $11.20 (1.0 = $1,120)	Second Friday of month before futures expire

*1/2¢/lb. for two nearby options and 1¢/lb. for deferreds when futures price is below 15¢/lb. (will be 1¢ for all contracts beginning with October 1984). When the futures contract price is 15¢-40¢ per lb., the increment will be 1¢ for two nearby months and 2¢ for deferred months. When the futures contract price is above 40¢, the increment will be 2¢ for two nearby months and 4¢ for deferred months.

Underlying futures contract	Contract size	Strike price increments	Minimum fluctuation	Expiration date

Commodity Exchange Inc. (COMEX)

Gold	100 troy oz.	Varies*	10¢/oz. = $10 (1.0 = $100)	Second Friday of month before futures expire

*$10/oz. below $300; $20/oz. $300-$500; $30/oz. $500-$800; $40/oz. above $800

Silver	5,000 troy oz.	50¢ between $5-$14.99/oz,; $1 above $15/ oz.	1/10¢/oz. = $5 (1.0 = $100)	Second Friday of month prior to futures month

MidAmerica Commodity Exchange

Gold	33.2 troy oz.	$10/oz.	10¢/oz. = $3.32 (1 = $33.20)	Second Friday of month prior to futures delivery

New York Cotton Exchange

Cotton	50,000 lb.	Nearest two delivery months: 1¢ up to 74¢/lb., 2¢ at 75¢/lb. and above.	1/100¢/lb. = $5 (1.0 = $500)	First Friday preceding delivery month

New York Futures Exchange

NYSE Composite Stock Index	500 × NYSE Composite Index	2 pt.	0.05 pt. = $25 (1.0 = $500)	Last trading day of underlying futures contract

Winnipeg Commodity Exchange

Gold (Calls only)	20 oz.	$20/oz.	10¢/oz. = $2 (1.0 = $20)	Six business days before delivery month

Options on Actuals

New options were being introduced as this issue was being put together so the following list may not be complete. Options on futures (see pages 134-135) re-quired Commodity Futures Trading Commission approval. U.S. options in the list below have gone through the Securities and Exchange Commission.

Underlying instrument	Contract months	Local trading hours	Contract size	Strike price increments	Minimum fluctuation

American Stock Exchange (AMEX)

Major Market Index (20 stocks)	Four sequential expiration months	10:00-4:10	100 × index value	5 pt.	Premium less than $3: 1/16; above $3: 1/8 (1.0 = $100)
(Same details apply to **AMEX Market Value Index, Computer Technology Index, Oil and Gas Index and Transportation Index**)					
U.S. Treasury Bills (90-day)	Mar/June Sept/Dec	9:00-3:00	$1 million principal	1 pt.	0.01 pt. = $25 (1.0 = $2,500)
U.S. Treasury Notes (10-year)	Feb/May Aug/Nov	9:00-3:00	$100,000	2 pt.	1/32 pt. = $31.25 (1.0 = $1,000)

Chicago Board Options Exchange (CBOE)

S&P 100 Stock Index	Four sequential months	9:00-3:10	100 × index	5 pt.	Premium less than $3: 1/16; above $3: 1/8. (1.0 = $100)
(Same details apply to **S&P Telephone Index and S&P Transportation Index**)					
S&P 500 Stock Index	Mar/June Sept/Dec	"	"	"	"
U.S. Treasury Bonds (12% and 10⅜%)	Mar/June Sept/Dec	8:00-2:00	$100,000	2 pt.	1/32 pt. = $31.25 (1.0 = $1,000)

Underlying instrument	Contract months	Local trading hours	Contract size	Strike price increments	Minimum fluctuation

New York Stock Exchange

Underlying instrument	Contract months	Local trading hours	Contract size	Strike price increments	Minimum fluctuation
NYSE Index	Next three months and then December cycle	10:00-4:10	100 × index	5 pt.	1/16 up to $3; 1/8 above $3 (1.0 = $100)
NYSE Telephone Index	Next three months and then January cycle	"	"	"	"

Pacific Stock Exchange

Underlying instrument	Contract months	Local trading hours	Contract size	Strike price increments	Minimum fluctuation
PSE Technology Index	Four sequential months	7:00-1:10	100 × index	5 pt.	1/16 (1.0 = $100)

Philadelphia Stock Exchange (PHLX)

Underlying instrument	Contract months	Local trading hours	Contract size	Strike price increments	Minimum fluctuation
Deutsche Mark	Mar/June Sept/Dec	8:30-2:30	DM 62,500	$0.01	$0.0001/DM = $6.25 (1.0 = $625)
Swiss Franc	Mar/June Sept/Dec	8:30-2:30	SF 62,500	$0.01	$0.0001/SF = $6.25 (1.0 = $625)
Canadian Dollar	Mar/June Sept/Dec	8:30-2:30	CD $50,000	$0.01	$0.0001/CD = $5 (1.0 = $500)
British Pound	Mar/June Sept/Dec	8:30-2:30	£12,500	$0.05	$0.0005/£ = $6.25 (1.0 = $125)
Japanese Yen	Mar/June Sept/Dec	8:30-2:30	JY 6,250,000	$0.01	$0.000001/ JY = $6.25 (1.0 = $625)
French Franc	Mar/June Sept/Dec	8:30-2:30	FF 125,000	$0.005	$0.00005/FF = $6.25 (1.0 = $1,250)
Gaming/Hotel Stock Index	Next three months and two deferred months	10:00-4:10	100 × index	5 pt.	1/16 (1.0 = $100)
Gold/Silver Stock Index	"	"	"	"	"

Underlying instrument	Contract months	Local trading hours	Contract size	Strike price increments	Minimum fluctuation

International Options Market (MOI)
Division of the Montreal Exchange*

(All times EST/EDT)

Underlying instrument	Contract months	Local trading hours	Contract size	Strike price increments	Minimum fluctuation
Gold	Feb/May Aug/Nov	Amsterdam: 4:30-10:30 Montreal: 9:00-2:30 Vancouver: 2:30-7:00	10 oz.	U.S. $25 under $500; $50 above $500	10¢/oz. = $1
Canadian Dollar	Mar/June Sept/Dec	Montreal: 9:00-2:30 Vancouver: 2:30-7:00	CD $50,000	U.S. $0.01	$0.0001/CD = $5
Deutsche Mark	Mar/June Sept/Dec	Montreal: 9:00-4:00	DM 25,000	U.S. $0.01	$0.0001/DM = $2.50
Swiss Franc	Mar/June Sept/Dec	Montreal: 9:00-4:00	SF 25,000	U.S. $0.01	$0.0001/SF = $2.50
British Pound	Mar/June Sept/Dec	Montreal: 9:00-4:00	£5,000	U.S. $0.05	$0.0005/£ = $2.50
Japanese Yen	Mar/June Sept/Dec	Montreal: 9:00-4:00	JY 2,500,000	U.S. $0.01	$0.000001/ JY = $2.50
Canadian Bonds	Mar/June Sept/Dec	Montreal: 9:00-4:00	CD $25,000	CD $2.50	Premium under $2: 5¢; above $2: 1/8

*Some options also traded on the European Options Exchange at the Amsterdam Stock Exchange and at the Vancouver Stock Exchange.

Toronto Futures Exchange

Underlying instrument	Contract months	Local trading hours	Contract size	Strike price increments	Minimum fluctuation
Silver	Mar/June Sept/Dec	9:30-2:30	100 oz.	$1 below $15/oz.; $2.50 from $15-$35/oz.	5¢ below $2; 12½¢ above $2

Toronto Stock Exchange

Underlying instrument	Contract months	Local trading hours	Contract size	Strike price increments	Minimum fluctuation
TSE 300 Index	Next three months	10:00-4:10	100 × index	$1	5¢ under $2; 1/8 above $2

MARGIN REQUIREMENTS

Commodity	OUTRIGHT		SPREAD		SPOT MONTH	
	Initial	Maintenance	Initial	Maintenance	Outright	Spread
Chicago Board of Trade						
Corn	1,000	750	250	250	15,000	15,000
Oats	500	400	100	100	9,000	9,000
Soybeans	3,000	2,000	750	750	30,000	30,000
Soybean Meal	2,000	1,500	300	300	17,500	17,500
Soybean Oil	1,500	1,000	200	200	11,000	11,000
Wheat	1,000	750	250	250	17,000	17,000
Plywood	700	400	300	200	20,000	20,000
Old Silver (5,000 oz.)	4,800	3,800	1,000	1,000	60,000	60,000
New Silver (1,000 oz.)	800	600	150	150	12,000	12,000
Certificate Delivery						
GNMA	3,000	2,000	200	200	75,000	75,000
Ginnie Mae Mort.	1,500	1,200	200	200	75,000	75,000
U.S. Treasury Bonds	1,750	1,500	300	300	75,000	75,000
CD	3,000	2,000	600	400	75,000	75,000
10 Year T-Notes	2,000	1,500	200	200	75,000	75,000
2 Year T-Notes	3,000	2,000	200	200	75,000	75,000
Gold (1 Kilo)	700	500	200	200	20,000	20,000
Heating Oil	1,300	1,000	250	250	35,000	35,000
Chicago Mercantile Exchange						
Feeder Cattle	900	600	400	200	31,000	31,000
Live Cattle	900	600	400	200	26,000	26,000
Live Hogs	800	500	500	300	17,000	17,000
Pork Bellies	1,500	1,200	400	200	30,000	30,000
Lumber	900	700	300	200	20,000	20,000
S & P 500	6,000	3,000	400	200	6,000	3,000
S & P 100	3,300	1,200	200	100	3,300	1,200
COMEX						
Copper	1,000	750	200	200	19,000	19,000
Gold	1,750	1,500	300	300	45,000	45,000
Silver	4,000	3,000	660	660	60,000	60,000
Aluminum	1,500	1,125	150	150	20,000	20,000
International Money Market						
British Pound	1,500	1,000	400	400	42,000	42,000
Canadian Dollar	900	700	400	400	80,000	80,000
Deutschemark	1,500	1,000	400	400	50,000	50,000
Japanese Yen	1,500	1,000	400	400	50,000	50,000
Mexican Peso	3,000	2,500	3,000	2,500	50,000	50,000
Swiss Franc	2,000	1,500	400	400	60,000	60,000
Gold	2,500	2,000	400	400	45,000	45,000
One-Year Treasury Bills	1,000	700	300	200	75,000	75,000
90-Day Treasury Bills	1,500	1,200	500	300	75,000	75,000
C.D.	1,500	1,200	500	300	75,000	75,000
Eurodollars	1,500	1,200	500	300	75,000	75,000
MidAmerica Commodity Exchange						
Corn (1M bu.)	200	150	50	50	3,000	3,000
Oats (1M bu.)	100	80	20	20	1,800	1,800
Soybeans	600	400	150	150	6,000	6,000
Wheat (1M bu.)	200	150	50	50	3,400	3,400
Live Cattle	450	300	100	100	13,000	13,000
Live Hogs	360	240	120	120	8,500	8,500
Gold (33.2 oz.)	700	500	100	100	15,000	15,000
Silver (1M oz.)	800	600	150	150	12,000	12,000
Treasury Bonds	875	750	100	100	25,000	25,000
Treasury Bills	1,250	1,000	100	100	25,000	25,000
Sugar	600	400	200	200	5,000	5,000
Rough Rice	750	500	50	50	18,000	18,000

New York Futures Exchange						
NYFE Comp. Index	3,500	1,500	200	100	6,000	3,000
New York Coffee, Sugar and Cocoa Exchange						
Cocoa	2,000	1,750	400	400	2,800	2,300
Coffee	1,500	1,125	500	400	45,000	25,000
Sugar 11	1,500	1,300	800	700	10,000	9,000
New York Cotton Exchange						
Cotton	1,500	1,125	500	500	35,000	35,000
Orange Juice	1,500	1,000	250	250	21,000	10,000
Propane	1,500	1,000	400	400	5,000	5,000
New York Mercantile Exchange						
Platinum	1,500	1,250	300	250	2,750	1,400
Round White Potatoes	500	375	250	175	1,750	1,750
Heating Oil	1,500	1,000	200	150	6,000	5,000
Leaded Gas	1,500	1,000	200	150	6,000	5,000
Palladium	1,250	1,000	250	175	3,000	3,000
Crude Oil	1,500	1,000	200	150	6,000	5,000
Kansas City Board of Trade						
Kansas City Wheat	1,000	750	100	100	17,000	17,000
Kansas City/Chicago Wheat			250	250		
Value Line	6,500	2,000	400	200	6,500	2,000

All statements made herein while not guaranteed, are believed to be reliable, and based on information considered to be accurate. The above listed margins are current and are however, <u>SUBJECT TO CHANGE WITHOUT NOTICE.</u>

4
How to Get Started in Futures Trading

Getting started in futures trading is easy. Many brokers (associated persons) are available to help you get started. You will find a list of futures brokers in the "yellow pages" of your telephone directory. The major firms regularly advertise in financial journals such as *Futures* Magazine. Or, you may already be in contact with a stock broker who can recommend someone in his firm to handle your futures program. Most major stock brokerage firms deal in futures. There also are many specialized brokerage firms which handle futures only.

Choosing a broker is an important decision. You need to feel confident with the broker. He should demonstrate a sincere interest in you. He will teach you some of the beginning concepts of trading if you are a beginner. You can start your selection process by walking into the offices of several firms to get acquainted with their futures personnel.

Chat with prospective brokers about the amount of trading capital you are willing to commit. If you plan to commit only $1,000 to the market in the beginning, the broker should know. He may not want to take the time to answer your questions for an account that small. It could be a mistake on his part, but it is a fact you should know early in your relationship. If the first broker sounds too busy to handle your small account, try another.

In your initial discussion with the broker, ask how long it takes to complete a transaction with his firm. Have him tell you how an order is handled. While you are in the interviewing process, you'll learn a little from each broker that could be helpful in selecting and making your first trade.

The broker you select should have a good idea of what type of money management philosophy you have. Are you in the game for the big trade — a "risk it all" attitude? Or are you willing to go slow, manage your risks and take your time waiting for the right trade? By the time you have completed this book, you will develop a feeling for your financial philosophy. Chapter 6 will be particularly useful in helping you decide how to approach the market. In your interviews with brokers, ask them about their trading philosophies — how do they select trades, how long do they hang on to winners and losers, etc.

What to Expect From Your Broker

You should expect a broker to execute your orders efficiently, give you timely confirmations of your purchases or sales and provide accurate monthly statements summarizing your trading activity.

You can expect your broker to have access to timely information that could influence your trade. That means his connections to the trading floor and to a wire service are important. He should subscribe to at least one set of futures price charts and several industry newsletters that give you a well-rounded view of major opinion leaders.

The broker you select should be willing to give you the names of other futures traders with whom you can verify the broker's qualifications. Ideally, you will choose a broker who deals only in futures, but there are exceptional stock brokers who handle a few futures accounts with great success. Your challenge is to find the person who is competent and willing to work with you during your learning process. Many brokerage firms have excellent literature that will help you, so ask each prospective broker what his firm offers in this area.

Once you have settled on the firm and your broker, you're ready to sign the account papers, write a check and make your first trade.

Many firms have a $5,000 minimum account. Some are higher. Some brokers refuse accounts under $10,000 because they prefer dealing with a few large accounts. Also, the discount brokers are attracting the business of many traders and many small accounts are now trading through discount brokers to cut costs.

You sign several forms when opening an account. You will have to supply personal and credit references, specify the type of account you are opening and supply instructions on where to send your statements. The customer agreement form authorizes your broker to liquidate your position if you fail to maintain certain minimum deposits. The risk disclosure forms acknowledge you recognize that you are taking a risk.

Margin Money and How It Works

The money you deposit in your account is called margin money — a security deposit that guarantees you will perform once you enter into a trade. The amount of margin money required depends on the commodity you are trading, the firm's rules, and sometimes the exchange's varying margin requirements. This is done to prevent overnight bankruptcies of firms caused by customers with large losses and insufficient margin in their account to cover the losses.

There are certain standards that normally hold true, however. For example, the typical margin is usually less than 10% of the value of the contract traded. With a 5,000-bu. contract of soybeans selling at $6, the margin seldom would be more than $3,000. A similar size corn contract usually requires $500 to $750. See the list of margin requirements from one firm on page 48 for examples of minimum margins. Remember these can change dramatically if market conditions change.

After you trade, you must meet certain financial requirements set by the commodity exchanges and brokerage firms.

Initial margin deposit. Each exchange has a minimum requirment for clearing member firms on how much cash must be deposited before you can begin trading. This deposit — or the margin — calls for a specific amount per contract traded and may vary depending on the commodity. As mentioned earlier, individual firms, for safety's sake, may require more than this minimum margin. Initial margin is the amount required in your account to execute your first trade.

Maintenance margin. Each exchange and clearing member firm also has a minimum acceptable level of equity balance you can carry per contract. Once your equity gets below your maintenance level, you receive a margin call. This simply means the market has moved against you, and as of today's prices, you now have insufficient money in your account to support your position. You are faced with putting additional margin money into your account. If you fail to deposit this money, your broker has the authority to close out (offset) your entire position.

Both the buyer and seller deposit margin money, which serves as a performance bond to insure that all contracts are settled. Clearing members of the futures exchanges have the responsibility for fulfilling contract commitments. If there is a default, the clearing firm through whom the defaulting party is dealing must come up with the deficit. That firm then will file suit or take whatever measures are necessary to collect the amount in default.

The broker you select will tell you what his firm's margin requirements are. That firm's requirements may vary from another firm's by several hundred dollars. But don't select a firm just because they ask for the lowest margin deposit. Margin deposits provide protection for you, too.

When you sign your account forms, you agree to maintain a certain minimum account balance. When you experience a loss that depletes your account below that minimum level, called a "maintenance level," you get a "margin call." That's simply a telephone call from your broker asking you to reestablish your minimum or to liquidate your position.

Many firms have a rule that once the market has moved against you enough to wipe out 25% of your margin, you must reestablish the full initial margin. You might have purchased a 1,000-bu. mini-contract of soybeans at $6 with the minimum deposit of $1,000. The day the market breaks to $5.75 your broker may ask for an additional $1,250 of margin money.

There are two ways to minimize margin calls:

1. Put more money into your account than the minimum. Some experts recommend that you never commit more than one-third of your trading capital on any given trade at any one time. That would mean opening an account with $3,000 if you wanted to trade a contract of soybeans with a $1,000 margin requirement.

2. Use "stop loss" orders that get out of a position "automatically" before you lose enough money to get a margin call. We will discuss this in greater detail later.

Types of Trading Accounts

There are several different types of accounts you may open to trade futures.

Regular trading account: This may be held in your name, in you and your spouse's name or your company name. You make the decisions in this account. You may consult your broker and others for advice, but you are held financially responsible for the activity in this account and for initiating and closing out trades.

Discretionary account: This account gives your broker discretion on when to make a trade. Some major misunderstandings have taken place over the years between trader and broker on accounts that were treated like discretionary accounts but were opened as regular accounts.

Discretionary accounts sometimes are called managed accounts or guided accounts. Under a discretionary account, you give full authority to the broker to trade for you. The guided or managed account appeals to the person who doesn't want to take the time to learn trading discipline himself.

Limited partnerships: Under this arrangement, several limited partners share profit and losses in a joint account. Each partner assumes only a limited amount of loss. As a limited partner, your loss is limited to the amount of investment made in the partnership. There are no margin calls. The general partner assumes unlimited risk and is paid a fee or percentage of the profit for providing that service. Limited partnerships and commodity funds usually rely on professional managers to devise the trading system and recommend specific trades.

Commodity pool, fund. Funds are similar to limited partnerships in that the individual risks only the amount he invests. (You can sometimes lose more money than you invest in a regular trading account. This happens when the market moves against you so fast that you are unable to get out before your entire account is liquidated.)

Futures funds are available through many brokerage firms and provide the advantage of pooling your capital with lots of other money so the techniques of money management can be used more efficiently. Frequently, small traders who were forced out of a position due to a loss feel they could have made large profits if they had a bit more "staying power" — the ability to hang on a few more days even if there is a loss in a position. Funds and limited partnerships have this staying power. But staying power is no guarantee of success. In fact, staying power sometimes is a detriment in that huge losses are allowed to accumulate.

For the purposes of this book, we are assuming you eventually will open a regular trading account where you make your own decisions. You will invest your own money in hopes of multiplying your risk capital by several hundred percent over a 2- or 3-year period.

With that assumption in mind, you need to be familiar with how trades are made, how to place your orders and how to develop a trading strategy ... all subjects for the next section and the following two chapters.

The Futures Contract

The bond between a futures market buyer and seller is the futures contract, a legally-binding agreement. The details of a contract are spelled out in various brochures of the exchanges. However, in trading futures, you do not actually sign a piece of paper at the time you enter an order. Instead, your commitment is recorded on your statement from the brokerage house. This statement is your agreement to either buy or sell on the terms of the contract traded at that particular futures exchange.

In a futures contract you agree either to deliver or accept a *given amount of the specified commodity during a specified period.* The contract spells out the quality and delivery conditions that the exchange establishes and which you must meet.

The futures contract binds you in two major areas: 1. You promise to make or accept actual delivery. (But before it is time to fulfill this commitment, you probably will make an offsetting transaction.) 2. You promise to put up and maintain a set amount of cash reserve in your account as long as the contract is open.

If a futures contract is allowed to run until termination date, the seller of that contract is required to deliver the commodity at the location specified by the contract. The buyer then must make a full cash payment and accept delivery based on the settlement price for that day. If you accepted delivery based on the settlement on 5,000 bu. of July corn at $3 on July 10, you would write a check to your broker for $15,000 plus a storage deposit. You would get a warehouse receipt and would own cash corn in a bin in Chicago. Of course, you could sell the corn later.

In reality, only 2% of the futures contracts are completed by making and taking delivery of the commodity. The other 98% are settled by an offset. In these offset situations, buyers and sellers enter the market before the day the contracts terminate and enter an order to offset their position. If a buyer had purchased 5,000 bu. of corn, he would offset by selling 5,000 bushels. A settlement price, and a net profit or loss, then is indicated on the statements the traders receive from the brokerage house.

How Futures Trades are Extended

Despite the seeming chaos in the pit of a futures exchange which seems to be the order of business to the casual observer, trading is done by people who are very professional in their jobs. People deal directly with one another — people who are intent on doing the best job they can for customers or themselves.

Orders from individual traders through brokerage houses come into order desks at an exchange. An order is taken over the phone and written on an order form. The time of the order is stamped, delivered by a "runner" to a broker on the trading floor. The floor broker shouts the order, "Sell 5,000 Dec. corn," and makes an appropriate hand signal. The response comes, "Buy!" Buyer and seller have met and agreed on the sale of a contract.

Both floor brokers record the contract terms on the order form. The data recorded includes the price, number and kind of contracts, and buyer and seller symbols, which designate the firms which concluded the transaction. The complete order then is returned to the order desk by the runner to be stamped again to show the time of the trade.

Before being recorded on a trading card, a docket is made of all trades by the broker that day.

The bottom copy of the form is returned to the phone operator, who reports back to the individual hedger or trader that the trade has been made.

All trading cards are turned in to keypunch operators who record all transactions on computer tape. Tapes are matched to be sure there are no mix-ups. This process happens hundreds of times each day in an orderly, efficient manner.

A futures exchange is really an extension of the village market. It's a place where buyers and sellers meet. The exchange does not buy or sell commodities. The main functions of a futures exchange are:

1. Providing accommodations for trading.
2. Establishing a method of delivery and the rules thereof.

3. Writing and enforcing the rules under which members and their employees conduct trading.
4. Distributing price quotations.
5. Representing trading members before the government and the public.

Memberships on a futures exchange range from about $20,000 for a seat on the smaller exchanges to over $300,000 on the major exchanges. They are sold on a bid and asked basis, except when new memberships are authorized. Individuals who hold memberships are able to trade at special member rates.

The Commodity Futures Trading Commission is the regulatory body, superceding the Commodity Exchange Authority. Its purpose is to license futures market exchanges and regulate them. The CFTC registers brokers and futures commission merchants, supervises trading, and regulates the total position that may be held by one individual. Between the regulation of the exchanges and the CFTC, the public is protected against collusion, price-fixing and price-manipulating.

5
Placing Your Order

Many costly mistakes are made every day by traders who give their brokers sloppy instructions. A clear order, understood by both you and your broker, eliminates misunderstanding that may result in large losses.

One of the best ways to make sure you have communicated clearly is to give the order to your broker, then ask him to repeat it. As he repeats the order, you write it down as a double check. It is easy to make costly verbal mistakes. One of the worst is saying "buy" when you are thinking "sell." The execution of a buy order when you mean sell could double the size of your position when you think you are liquidating it entirely.

Each order must include the following elements: Name of the futures contract and, if necessary, the exchange; whether you want to buy or sell; number of contracts (or thousands of bushels in the case of grains and soybeans); delivery month; and price instructions. "Buy 2 Feb Comex gold at the market" is the type of order that summarizes everything you want to do.

The Price Element of Your Order

There are several different types of orders you can use to specify the price at which you are willing to accept a trade:

Market order. The one order most traders use is to buy or sell "at the market." "Market" orders are executed at the best possible price obtainable at the time the order reaches the pit. Example: "Sell 2 Dec T-bills at the market."

Market if touched. This order also tells the broker to buy or sell "at the market" but only after the price has reached a specified level. A "market-if-touched" (MIT) order to buy is placed below the current price. If the price comes down to it, the MIT order is "touched off" and becomes a market order. Example: If May pork bellies are at 55.00, the order might be, "Buy 2 May bellies at 54.50, MIT."

Fill or kill. This order, in addition to having a specific time element, also has a specified limit price. If the broker cannot get this price immediately, the order is cancelled.

Or-better orders. "OB" orders are used to purchase or sell futures at a designated price or better. If it is an OB order to buy, the price designated must be above the current market price; if it is an OB order to sell, the price designated must be below the current market price. The OB order tells the floor broker that you realize the present market is at a better price but that he has some range in price to make sure you get your order executed. Foreign traders use this type of order because they realize it might take several minutes before their order can reach the trading floor.

An OB order also might be used on the opening. It tells the broker that you are willing to pay up to a specified level, although your order may be filled at a better level than your OB price allows.

Stop order. A stop order instructs your broker to enter your order at the market when the market reaches a specific price. A stop order is called a "stop loss" order when it is placed to close out a position in the event prices move against you. In this case, the order is entered with the intention of minimizing your loss or perhaps locking in a profit.

Stop orders can be entered either as a "buy stop" or a "sell stop." A buy stop tells your broker to execute an order if the price of the commodity rises to a particular level. For example, if you want to buy December sugar when the price reaches 10¢ per lb., you tell your broker you want to place a "buy stop" at 10¢ per lb. If this is given to him on an open basis, whenever the market reaches that point, you are "stopped into the market."

A "sell stop" order tells your broker to execute on order when the price falls to a given level, at which point it is to be executed "at the market." Because you are giving your broker the opportunity to execute "at the market," your order will not necessarily be executed at the specific price. If market trading is hectic that day, your trade might be slightly above or below your sell point.

Stop orders may be used to avoid a loss, protect a profit or establish a new position. On your order to buy sugar at 10¢ per lb., you might instruct your broker to sell it if it falls below 9.50¢ per lb. That way, you limit your loss to 50 points. In case sugar rises from your buy point at 10¢ to 11¢, you could raise your sell order to 10.5¢ and lock in a profit.

Another variation of the stop order is to move the stop up or down with the market. Say, for example, that you have a profit in your sugar at 11¢ and the market continues to move higher. You may want to move your stop 50 points under the market's close each day. You are, therefore, locking in a larger and larger profit as the market continues to move higher. This technique is called a "trailing stop." It has great appeal to beginning traders because it is a protection device. The major problem with a trailing stop is that if it is placed too close to current prices, you can be stopped out of the market just before the futures make a substantial move. So, the placement of these stops is extremely important and should be discussed with your broker as a part of your trading strategy.

Stop limit order. If you are worried that your stop order might give you an unfavorable price, you can place a limit on what you are willing to pay with a "stop limit order." This order may contain two price instructions, one to indicate when the order is to be activated as a market order and a second price to indicate the limit you will pay. Example: "Buy 1 Feb belly at 55.00 stop 55.20 limit." That means your broker will try to buy a February pork belly at 55.00 and that he may go as high as 55.20. If possible, of course, he will buy it for less, but he will not buy above 55.20.

This type of order usually is not necessary and may prevent you from getting your order executed. But if your stop order is at a place where there may be a number of other stop orders, you may want to put a limit on the price you'll pay to prevent getting a bad fill on your order.

The Time Element of Your Order

Besides price, you must specify a time element when you talk to your broker.

Day order. The "day order" is one which is good only the day it is placed. If not executed, a day order expires at the close of the trading day and is cancelled automatically. Example: Let's say you are buying 5,000 bu. of December corn futures. You enter a day order to buy at $3.01 when the market is trading $3.04. Your order will be executed only if the market trades lower and hits $3.01. If you enter a day order and the market doesn't trade as low as $3.01, the order is automatically killed at the close of trading.

Open order. An "open" order remains in effect until it is filled or until you cancel it. Let's assume you entered the order to buy December corn at $3.01 and it took two weeks for the market to fall enough to hit $3.01. The moment there was a sufficient volume of trading to fill your order, it would be executed at $3.01.

Good until cancelled. This type of order is, in effect, the same as an open order.

Good until (date). You can modify an open order by saying, "This order is good until Sept. 15," or "This order is good until 10:30 this morning." Orders placed with time limits are automatically killed if not filled within that time period.

Fill or kill. The "fill or kill" order is sometimes called a "quick order." It is an order that must be executed at the specific price you ask for, or at a better price, immediately. As soon as the order reaches the pit, it is offered. If the market is not trading at that price, the order is killed or cancelled.

On the opening or close. You may instruct your broker to try to execute your order on the opening or close of the market. This means it must be executed in the two or three minutes of trading at one of the extreme ends of the day. If not filled then, the orders are cancelled. "Opening only," "market on close" and "stop-close only" are terms for orders of this type. Not all exchanges accept this type of order.

Combination Orders and How They Work

A combination order is one which has two possible executions: If the first order is executed, the second one is cancelled. For example, you may want to buy corn if it reaches $3.10 per bushel. However, if the market drops to $2.90, you may want to sell corn. You could enter a combination order to buy at $3.10 or sell at $2.90 on the basis of "one cancels other" (OCO). This means that if you bought the corn at $3.10, your order to sell at $2.90 would be cancelled automatically. Some brokers will not accept combination orders that involve two commodities because they cannot physically be in two trading pits at the same time.

A contingent order is a variation of the combination order in that your order is executed based on some fact happening. For example, you may want to buy one July pork belly at the market when August pork bellies sell above $60. This order is used when you believe one contract of bellies will set the tone for the entire market.

Other Types of Orders

"Scale orders" can be used to establish or liquidate positions while the market is moving up or down. For example, you may say you want to buy six contracts of August pork bellies beginning at $56, with an additional purchase every dollar higher. After the position has been fully executed, a "scale-down" order could be used to liquidate those six contracts. These orders are used to spread buying and selling over a wider price period to avoid the mistake of putting all your positions on or taking all of your positions off at any given price.

A "spread order" is an order to take advantage of the difference in price or "spread" between two different contract months, two different markets, such as Chicago and Minneapolis, or two different commodities. Whenever you enter a spread order, the buy portion of the order always is given first.

An "intermarket spread" might involve buying a contract of May wheat in Chicago and selling a contract of May wheat at Minneapolis. An "intracommodity" spread would be buying one Chicago May wheat and selling one Chicago July wheat. An "intercommodity" spread would be an order to buy one May wheat and sell one May corn.

It's a good idea to discuss with your broker the types of orders you intend to use as a part of your overall trading plan.

6
How to Apply Money Management Strategies

You may boost your trading profit by gleaning ideas on money management from the managers of big stock and futures portfolios who have access to computers. The more money you have, the better the techniques of "money management" work. But, even with $1,000 to $5,000, you can use some of their professional techniques.

"Intuition" and "feel of the market" have had to make room for a newcomer in the trading world: computer portfolio management. The computer system originated among portfolio managers of stock investment funds, who sought a structured money-management approach to spreading risk. Now, futures fund managers are harnessing dozens of computer systems to increase futures trading discipline — and, hopefully, reduce risks.

Instinctive nonscientific traders, who often play it big when they have a "hot hand," enjoy telling horror stories of early computer systems that simply kicked out buy and sell signals. Often, the primitive system looked great at first, then went berserk when the market changed complexion, causing its followers to lose large sums.

But the newer computer programs are more sophisticated. Unlike a hunch-playing professional who often risks a higher percentage of his trading capital on a single trade, the new systems integrate buy-sell signals with the individual's risk-bearing ability.

That concept defends the trader against two vicious enemies: emotional trading and overtrading.

The new computer systems have five main principles which even a small trader can use to a certain extent. The money management philosophy provides discipline and improves your trading odds. Most brokerage firms have computerized systems, funds and managed account programs which bring some or all of these money management ideas to even the beginner trader. We present these techniques to encourage the beginner "to take a page" from the large fund manager's success book.

Spread Risks With A "Portfolio"

You should trade a portfolio of several futures at a time, avoiding the potential for a wipeout on a single position. Diversification also spreads your financial net wider, increasing your odds of catching the "big mover" — the trend that more than doubles in value.

Computer models can select the warmest prospects for your portfolio. With the strongest prospects sorted out, the portfolio manager can do a more thorough job of watching for the real movers among them. This approach gives you a better chance of being aboard when the big move starts.

Computer models generally weed out low-volume commodities. If less than 250 contracts trade daily, you face difficulty getting execution. A stop order, particularly, may be filled several points or several hundreds of dollars away from the last trade in such a thin market.

Obviously, it takes a lot of money to trade eight to ten commodities. A $20,000 trading budget is minimal. Equity of $50,000 gives you more flexibility; $100,000 of trading capital takes full advantage of the portfolio concept. Thus, the real protection of portfolio trading isn't available to most individual speculators unless they pool their capital with others in commodity funds or limited partnerships.

A few funds and limited partnerships have shown consistently good performances. You can check the prospectus of a fund at brokerage offices to size up your odds of trading success with a fund versus trading your own account.

If you are considering a futures fund, take a good look at the record of the fund advisors to see if they have been consistently successful in the past. If not, "buyer beware."

Some funds are structured so the advisor *must* churn your account to get his bonus. That is a red flag if you're considering pooling your capital in a fund or limited partnership. If you have to give up too many advantages for the privilege of pooling your money, you may be better off taking your chances or waiting until you accumulate at least $5,000 of trading capital. That's about the minimum level where a small portfolio becomes practical.

Carry a Large Financial Margin

Maintain a safe excess margin. One of the major pitfalls in futures trading is that speculators get so fired up in a particular trade they put all their risk capital into a single position. If the trade goes sour, it scrubs out the trader's entire financial reserve.

Money managers suggest you carry 10% of the value of each contract traded in your margin account. In other words, if you were trading one contract of soybeans, you would take 10% times the price, say $7 a bu., times the contract size of 5,000 bu., or $3,500. If you had eight contracts in a portfolio with each valued about like the soybean contract, you would need $28,000 (8 × $3,500).

To be sure you have adequate capital, some managers would take double that amount and put the excess into Treasury bills to draw interest. With this kind of approach, you can stay with a losing position longer if your trading system says "stay." Even if your first several trades show losses, you have "staying power."

Carrying a large margin excess doesn't mean you let a losing trade slide until it swallows the full 10% reserve. Stop loss orders can minimize your losses on each trade. The reserve helps you consistently stick with your strategic buy and sell signals, rather than breaking discipline and falling back on emotion.

Take Only the Good Trades

Select good trades. Before you pick the specific trades, you need to select those trending futures which give you the best chance to ride some big moves. The objective of money managers is to find futures that break out of congestion areas and make major moves in one direction before reversing. Systems that take advantage of even 20% to 50% of these big moves can make money. So, the key is to select futures with trending characteristics and to catch the key "breakouts."

Money managers are frustrated by markets that trade sideways in congestion areas. It's easy to get "whipsawed" (buying at the top of a trading range and selling at the bottom, only to have the market go back up again).

Over the long pull, futures with good trading characteristics include cattle, hogs, soybeans, coffee and cocoa. When these markets "break out" of a congestion area, they usually make a move large enough to trade with less threat of a quick whipsaw. Long-term price charts help you see which commodities make such trending moves. Computer programs are ideally suited to screen out futures with this behavior.

You can't always pick the best-trending futures. That's why, if you have the capital to trade several, you increase your chances of getting two or three good trades out of eight or ten traded. The more capital you have, the less pressure there is to get the right trades early in the game.

If you are right in your trade selection only 50% of the time, you can be a big winner if you have taken advantage of some big trending profits while minimizing your losses.

Following a Trading System

Picking the right trading system which imposes rules on your market entry and exit is the next important step, because the system can help you cut your losses short. Most money managers use modified versions of point-and-figure or moving average systems to generate buy or sell signals. If you objectively study bar charts, you can visually spot breakouts and gain some of the same advantages.

Computer trading systems enhance traditional charting techniques in two ways. First, the computer can test several trading techniques against a given futures past performance. Second, it can select the particular buy-sell rule which is working best currently. For instance, it can choose the best combination of moving averages, depending on the market's volatility.

The optimum system is one sensitive enough to detect a reversal but not so sensitive that it whipsaws you and generates high commission costs.

If you're willing to substitute your own time and thought for a computer program, you can go a long way toward selecting the system that generates the best buy-sell signals in a given market.

You can subscribe to commodity price chart services, which do the basic work of keeping up-to-date charts on many futures. You can look through the record to see which systems have been performing well on the futures you plan to trade. An investment of $200 to $500 per year in chart services may go a long way toward making up for not having access to a computer. In fact, some relatively simple point-and-figure or moving average trading systems have been highly profitable when put in the hands of a disciplined trader who consistently follows the system's rules.

Become a Disciplined Trader

Exercise trading discipline. Many traders become losers because they can't follow a plan. After a couple of losses, they become emotional, abandon their basic game plan and begin "taking shots" at the market. The result is usually disastrous. Traders who stick to a set of trading rules have a better shot at becoming big winners. *Trading discipline is probably more important than the trading system you choose.*

Discipline means shutting out emotions. It means becoming mechanical in making trades when certain price action occurs. Disciplined traders don't take their profits too early, and they keep their losses short by trading with a set of guidelines that tells them when to abandon a position. Here's where a mechanical or computerized system has the advantage over a less organized approach.

"We know that if we follow a strict set of rules, we'll stay out of trouble and make money," says Chris Fund, a commodity manager from Lafayette, Ind., who regularly uses computer aids to provide buy and sell signals. "The computer simulation tells us we can expect losses in some commodities. When we know what to expect, we aren't as tempted to second-guess the system."

Do-It-Yourself Discipline

Although the computer carries more variables and reacts to more sophisticated trading rules, you don't need a computer in your own living room to improve your profit potential. You just need to follow your own trading rules strictly. Your broker can help you determine your "game plan" or trading system. Many computer systems are available to individual traders. Some are offered on a subscription basis by advisory services; others are offered on a "managed account" basis. You may want to subscribe to a service that has a systematic approach to trading.

Money management concept	What it means	If you have $1,000 to invest . . .	If you have $5,000 to invest . . .
1. Balanced portfolio	Diversification of your funds over several commodities.	With only $1,000 to invest, you lack margin to spread over several commodity trades. This tool is unavailable to small traders.	Diversification over four commodities is practical, if low-margin or mini-contracts are traded.
2. Excess margin	Buying time by giving the market "room to work."	Again, $1,000 is not enough to hold a reserve of trading capital. You risk almost all of your trading capital on each trade.	Limited use of this tool because your trading capital is exposed if you trade four commodities. However, it is still possible to keep perhaps $1,000 in reserve.
3. Trade selection	Investing in "trending commodities."	Trade selection is critical, but with only $1,000 you have little room to make mistakes. Must wait for "high odds" trades. Fewer trades are suitable.	Failure to catch trends early wipes out capital. Can't give trades a chance to go against you.
4. Trading system	Working a plan that gives you consistent results.	Your system of trading is vital. Yet most systems which require giving the market room to work are not available to you.	Selection of system is limited to those which cut losses short; increasing odds of eating up capital in commissions.
5. Discipline	Enforcing other principles systematically.	The need for success on trades adds emotional pressure; makes disciplined trading difficult.	Capital shortage still threatens your discipline.
	Comment	The highest percent of losers are in this category. Lack of trading capital renders most of the tools of money management ineffective.	Chances of success much higher if losses are cut. Lack of discipline is biggest threat at this level. You may improve your odds by "pooling" your money in a fund.

If you have $20,000 to invest . . .	If you have $50,000 to invest . . .	If you have $100,000 to invest . . .
Six-commodity portfolio is practical, possibly 8-10 using mini-contracts.	An eight-commodity portfolio is practical; 10 with some mini-contracts.	A 10-commodity portfolio is practical. You get full benefit of this tool.
Equity is sufficient for some capital reserve. Probably risk 50%-75% of your capital on open trades at this level.	You can easily hold risk to 25% to 50% of your capital, even lower with mini-contracts or systems with moderate stop losses.	Only 10%-15% of your capital is exposed on open positions. Full benefit of this tool is available to you.
You can afford more losers. You have better chance of profit because your stop losses don't have to be as close.	You have the full use of trade selection advantage here because half your trades can go sour and still be a winner under the right system.	No limits to type of trades. Adequate capital to ride with bad trades longer; reduces chance of "churning."
More trading systems are practical because you have adequate capital to stay with a position longer.	You can employ systems that aren't so sensitive that you chew your account to death. Much wider selection of systems available.	Systems are the key to returns, assuming good discipline is right.
As more commodities are traded, need for strict discipline increases.	Mechanical or computer systems are ideal to enforce your discipline at this level.	Discipline pays its biggest advantage. Big losses at this level are probable without trading by strict rules.
The enemies, capital shortage and emotion are reduced. Odds of being a winner are increased 3-4 times over a $5,000 investment.	Money isn't your problem here. Profits limited to skillful use of the management tools.	Losses at this level are usually associated with putting too much money on too few positions.

7
Forecasting Price Moves Through Fundamental Analysis

You make profitable trades by accurately forecasting the effects of various market factors on price. Fundamental analysts believe in this approach and apply the economic rule of demand and supply to forecast prices. They operate on the fundamental rule that any factor which decreases the supply or increases the use of a commodity tends to boost prices. Any factor which increases the supply or decreases the use tends to cause an increasing stockpile and decreases price.

Many of the top money winners in futures look at futures from both fundamental and technical angles. (The technical approach is covered in the following chapters.) Each trading approach can confirm the other, complement the other and add more certainty to a trade. The higher the probability of taking a correct position at the outset of a move, the lower the risk.

Although some traders scoff at the fundamental analyst, why wear a set of glasses with only one lens? Why not use the advantages provided by both good fundamental and good technical analysis?

Many traders shy away from fundamentals because they demand effort and time. But most speculators end up losers just because they think the market will yield profits without concentration and patience. Nothing comes easy in futures trading.

"But I don't want to become an economist of demand and supply; what do I know about gold bullion or pork bellies?" you ask. Learning does not come easily, but much information is free of charge from government sources such as the U.S. Department of Agriculture (USDA). Good information can indicate trends and profit opportunities.

Build Your Confidence and Futures Knowledge

The best way to develop fundamental analysis skills is to concentrate on one futures or a related group or "complex." Once you know the ground rules, you can critically assess the situation for almost any futures. And you get an important side benefit: A sensitivity to the overall movement of futures warns you about impending inflation or deflation, a key to profitable investments in any area of the economy.

With a good grasp of the fundamentals, you can double-check recommendations from your marketing service or newsletter. Some top-notch traders take certain newsletters, not because they are infallible, but because they give the keys to the fundamental outlook for a commodity. And they give fundamental news before it moves price. Good fundamental advice provides the backdrop for the most profitable trades.

A futures market unfortunately can no longer be considered in a vacuum. The larger influences of world business cycles and currency appreciation or depreciation must be worked into your strategy.

How Not To End Up Correct But Poor

Many good traders respect and use the supply and demand situation to their advantage. Fundamental analysis tells you when prices should be high or low, based on seasonal tendency and the causes of a tight or ample supply. But knowledge of economic factors will not time your trades, protect your profits or manage your trading stake. No matter what the approach, protecting your positions and timing your entry and exit are the essence of high-profit trading.

The big drawback of fundamental analysis is that, unlike a mechanical system, it requires a great deal of subjective judgment. You must not fall in love with your conclusions about the direction prices will take.

Good fundamental (supply/demand) analysis contributes to trading confidence if it is kept simple. You can keep it simple if you isolate the critical variables and weigh their importance in influencing price movements. For example, during the growing period of a crop commodity, the market responds more to supply than demand developments. Important demand developments may be overlooked due to the lopsided interest in the upcoming harvest.

Avoid confusing yourself in a whirlpool of fundamental facts. Early in your trading you should learn to judge the important price-moving factors and concentrate on them. You must, of course, have the confidence to lean against the wind of general opinion once you have decided. Often, the best trades are positions taken counter to the "consensus."

An advantage of fundamental analysis is that it can position you in a market nearer the bottom or top of a move than can technical analysis. Some excellent trades develop while prices trade sideways, showing no apparent direction. Knowledge of the fundamentals of a futures, its seasonal tendency and supply and demand balance can point up or down on the charts before the move surfaces through other forms of analysis.

One of the most common attacks on fundamental analysis is that all the information is already bid into the market price. Nothing could be farther from the truth. There is sometimes considerable lag between information on supply and demand and its full price impact. A situation evident in the fundamentals of a futures may take months or even years to work into price. Again, the difficulty often is not outguessing the market but having the courage and sound money management to be there when the price move finally takes off.

Estimating the Tightness of Supply

One critical fundamental fact for many futures is an estimate of the carryover or the amount "left over" at the end of a marketing year. The size of these ending stocks, be they 400-oz. gold bars or bushels of corn, says something about the strength or weakness of prices in the future. A large carryover in relation to expected production and use means sluggish prices. The carryover indicates whether supply is tight and will be rationed or is ample and will pressure prices lower.

Projections of ending stocks rise or fall on the level of projected demand and production. With the exception of some non-inventory commodities such as livestock, keeping a constant watch on stock levels gives a good clue to price level. Even in the case of livestock, the inventory of breeding animals and numbers on feed helps to forecast meat production in subsequent quarters.

The carryover method is a simple accounting formula: Beginning stocks plus production and net imports minus consumption equals ending stocks. If ending stocks (supply of the product) are at an historically low share of consumption and are declining year to year, prices should firm up during the marketing period. If stocks are historically high, a bear (lower) market should develop.

Ending stocks as a percentage of consumption or production is a common way to sum up the fundamental outlook for a commodity. Stocks also can be expressed in the number of days, weeks or months of supply remaining at the end of the season or marketing period at current usage rates. In the case of grains, a minimum pipeline supply must be maintained between old and new crops. If ending stocks are going to be too low, the market will ration current demand rates by a swift runup in prices.

When your analysis forecasts a situation like this, you earn a profit by buying futures contracts at the current price and selling them higher later.

Outguess Commodity Users and Official Reports

In using carryover analysis, other complications also must be considered. The size of the oncoming crop may be more important than the current carryover, for example. If it is sufficiently large, buyers may stand back from the market and purchase their inventory on a hand-to-mouth basis, intending to stock up with the cheaper-priced new crop. On the other hand, if the buyers miscalculate, the price of the commodity may run up smartly during harvest, normally a period of seasonal weakness.

The speculative game involves anticipating official reports which occur periodically throughout the marketing year. For example, as a crop season progresses, estimates of ending stocks change. Perhaps weather has trimmed yield expectations or economic boom has increased buying power from overseas customers.

Once the relative scarcity of a commodity is quantified through ending inventory, the fundamentalist then must assess current price levels. Are prices over- or under-valuing the commodity? Determining the relative value of a commodity is as important as market timing in making profits or losses on a trade. Of course, distortions may exist and not be rectified for weeks or months.

Fundamental Analysis Explains Price Action

Viewed purely from the position of price fluctuation, good fundamental analysis breaks out the components of price into various trends, ranging from seasonal movement (harvest lows followed by rising prices) to long-term trends (increasing or decreasing acreage, trends in the dollar, effects of crop substitution and technology).

A good knowledge of seasonal tendencies of a commodity, both futures and cash, plus a grasp of longer-term trends, such as expansion or contraction of livestock cycles and the business cycle, can aid your perception of future price levels relative to current prices. Correct analysis of these price differentials yield the biggest profits in futures trading.

An understanding of normal seasonal trends of a commodity gives the trader a set of expectations about price movement. A common mistake of beginning traders is to assume the points during the year for lows and highs in the cash market will match up with lows or highs in futures. The futures market is an anticipatory market and lows in the cash market may be anticipated by several weeks or months.

Although we will deal in more detail with different futures groups later, look at the wheat illustrations as an example of the effects of longer-term cycles. Note the decline in wheat acreage in 1977-1979 precipitated a reversal of a multi-year downtrend in cash wheat prices.

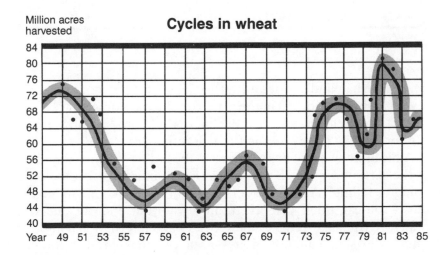

Also, note that price lows normally occur around harvest time in mid-summer within the longer-term trends. This is the type of typical seasonal pattern fundamental traders expect.

Chasing the Elusive Value Factor

The fundamentalist must compare his estimate of a reasonable price for a commodity with the current price level. Have prices made their seasonal lows? Has the market discounted the price too

Wheat Prices Received by Farmers

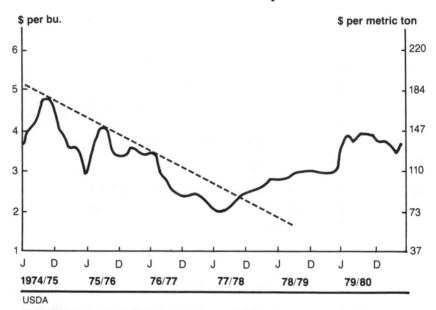

USDA
Source: USDA's Wheat Situation

heavily? What kind of price advance can be expected once seasonal lows have been made? Will the price roll sideways or advance? Are longer-term influences such as declining world production likely to firm or weaken prices during the marketing year?

A big unknown that has surfaced in the last few years is the value of the currency in which the futures is denominated. Is the dollar rising or falling? As one trader of a major grain company points out, "You can think you are trading grain but find out that you really are trading foreign exchange rates and international interest rates. The skill you use in this area can make the difference between profits or losses on international grain transactions." Because world trade accounts for the price-making share of many commodities, the dollar's effect on a commodity's value is critical.

Although fundamental analysts take their major price clues from supply and demand, most successful traders use other tools as well. Some traders rely upon years of experience in trading a particular market and have confidence as to how prices will respond to changes in fundamental factors.

Often, traders effectively employ fundamental analysis by taking a position opposite from the crowd and watching for short-term trades that correct speculative excesses in a trend. Remember, even though the fundamentalist can be "friendly" (or, expecting prices to go higher) on a commodity, all the bullishness may be bid into price.

More than once, prices have declined following a bullish crop report that turned out to be no more bullish than the trade already expected. Studies have shown price trends established prior to major U.S. crop reports tend to continue after the effect of the reports has been played out in the short-term.

A New Breed: The Computer Fundamentalist

In the last few years, technological advances in computer hardware and software programs have been applied to both the fundamental and technical approaches. But the computerization of fundamental analysis still requires a measure of judgment. You cannot forecast futures prices if you cannot explain past price behavior.

Computer-based projections of futures prices that employ fundamental analysis range from complex models that crank in thousands of variables to a simple equation that relates the price of a commodity to a few key demand and supply statistics.

Theoretically, the more variables included, the more complete your "picture" of a market should become. But complex equations often compound errors of fact and the relation of facts. Also, judgment is needed to restrict the number of years for which statistics are available.

Computer price forecasting involves an endless process of adjusting results. Every workable model includes many "levers" that can be pulled to correct patent absurdities in the results. Dr. Lawrence Klein of Wharton is one of the pioneers in computerized economic forecasting. He likens his model's price forecasts to a "troubleshooting" device to test the realism of the model in the marketplace. Forecasts become a reality check for abstract economic thinking.

Some critics of computerized price forecasting accuse the model builders of having a "black box" — that is, of hiding their opinions about price movement behind a screen of formulae and equations. This accusation probably is not fair, but certainly subscribers to these computer services adjust the assumptions and use a great deal of artful interpretation to arrive at a price outlook for a commodity.

Computer Price Forecasting In Action

A computer model that forecasts prices makes simplified assumptions about markets and their interrelationships. These relationships are weighted and are based on historical time series. Delayed responses to supply and demand changes are worked into the outcome through mathematical equations.

For instance, a large-scale agricultural model breaks down into clusters of blocks or commodity complexes. Grain or livestock complexes are analyzed on a quarterly basis and related to annual crop production estimates. Prices and stocks of a commodity are estimated two years into the future. The crop complex interacts with the livestock complex. These two commodity blocks knock against each other to produce a read-out of the state of the farm economy. A total farm income block then interacts with the rest of the model of the U.S. economy.

A computer printout based on fundamental factors may never replace seasoned judgment and a sharp sense of the market's mood. No matter how much you pay to have a commodity analysis, you must live with the decision you make and the losses or gains incurred. Therefore, an independent judgment based on knowledge of a market is crucial to building confidence and making the rapid decisions required in commodity trading.

Know the Peculiarities of Your Futures

The discussion in this chapter has been somewhat general and does not unravel all the intricacies of each market traded on futures exchanges. Nevertheless, you should be aware of some basic differences between futures if you want to apply fundamental analysis correctly.

The two dominant groups in U.S. farm commodities are live-stock and grains. These two sectors influence one another. Both are affected in the short and long term by weather developments. Unfortunately, there is little evidence that long-term weather projections have any great reliability. "Anyone who trades on long-range weather forecasts deserves what he gets," quips one weather consultant.

Political decisions can determine floors and ceilings on prices in domestic markets and world trade. Political decisions may determine the level of world demand, particularly in planned economies. For example, the decision by the Soviet government to buy grain abroad in the early 1970s increased world grain trade considerably and cleaned out U.S. government reserve stocks. Political decisions also influence acreage whether it be in the closed societies of the Soviet Union or the set-aside and PIK programs in the U.S. Furthermore, the political decisions in the United States to impose an embargo on grain shipments has immediate impact on grain demand and acreage.

The use of weather analysis tilts the odds farther in your favor. Dry soil conditions prior to planting support a case for a shortfall in crop production. If conditions begin to improve, such a development can be factored into an estimate of the potential for a summer weather rally. The market, for example, may have bid in too much weather concern. Weather cannot be predicted, but odds on certain outcomes given certain conditions are available and useful. It is another tool of the fundamentalist. Profitable trading doesn't always entail being right but, rather, tipping the odds in your favor.

Livestock Linked to Grains

Outlooks for grains affect the outlook for livestock. If your forecast calls for lower feed prices under a favorable weather scenario, then you can expect feeder cattle prices to move higher. When the livestock numbers are expanding and corn prices explode, as happened in 1974, meat prices are likely to collapse. In turn, you can expect a scarcity of market weight animals will develop so cattle and hog prices eventually will rebound sharply.

Over the longer pull, feed usage should increase with expanding on-feed numbers, a friendly trend for feedgrains. If wheat prices are price competitive with corn, then wheat — normally a food grain — may move into feed troughs in greater quantities. Cold winters also increase feeding rates.

A major impact of weather on grains is in export markets. The health of grain exports can make or break prices when carryover is down to relatively lean levels.

Exports compete directly with domestic demand for the free surplus of grains. That free surplus is the quantity over and above that held back on farms for feeding to animals and that portion entered into government storage programs, if any are in effect.

The important point to keep in mind is that foreign demand for U.S. grains depends on supplies elsewhere in the world and on the level of production in importing countries. Therefore, world weather can make or break world demand. If importing countries have bad crops, they must import to cover their food deficit. This fact has more importance than price and currency fluctuations.

Know the Difference Among Grains

Although the grain markets affect one another, they behave differently from each other because each responds to special market conditions.

In the 1970s, corn exports expanded dramatically. During the 1950s and '60s, corn was distinguished from wheat and soybeans because it was largely a domestic market like hogs and cattle. About half of the corn produced in the U.S. still remains on the farm to be fed to livestock. The other half is a residual which is bid for by government storage programs in periods of glut and by domestic industrial users, commercial feedlots and exporters. The lack of actual, free supplies has a leverage effect on prices greater than carryover would indicate.

Soybeans compete with corn in feed usage, to some extent, but the soybean market differs greatly from the corn market:

• Farmers do not use a significant volume of soybeans on the farm; virtually all the production enters the cash grain market directly.

• The premium of the cash price over the loan rate under government support programs has been historically wide and volatile.

• The Brazilian harvest in March-April has shifted the seasonal top in the bean market back from its former mid-summer peak.

• Exportable soybeans, unlike wheat or even corn, are grown in only two areas of the world.

• Although soybean oil has several fats and oils competitors, soybean meal as a livestock feed has few substitutes. Meal at times has almost twice the price effect on soybeans as does oil.

• Demand for soybeans in the domestic market is a function of the spread of crush margin between products and whole beans. If the product value from soybeans does not exceed the cost of beans by a sufficient amount, crushers will shut down. Normally, a bushel of soybeans yields 48 lbs. of meal and 11 lbs. of oil.

Wheat is a special case among the grains because it has been under artificial price supports by the U.S. government for many years. Demand for U.S. wheat has been a residual demand; buyers turn to U.S. wheat only when other world suppliers are sold out.

Wheat, moreover, is grown worldwide and has a history of less volatile price movement. Most of the wheat produced is consumed in the country of origin. Export demand picks up only when unfavorable weather reduces crops abroad, in which case price is no object because wheat has no immediate substitute aside from rice.

Some general conclusions can be drawn about the price movement of the three major grains: Corn prices are affected immediately by shifts in the level of exports while the effect of production changes on prices extends over a much longer time frame. To an extent, this is true for all the grains. Wheat is a bottom-builder, which means prices require a long period in which to bottom.

Agricultural commodities, in general, are dominated by the annual production cycle in the northern hemisphere. Contrary to the nature of the markets for industrial products, agricultural prices adjust to supply, not supply to prices. Because of the nature of agricultural supply and demand, small changes in either side of the balance, given modest carryover, can affect prices drastically.

Tracking the Food Group

The food futures complex involves mainly tropical or subtropical products such as orange juice, cocoa, sugar and coffee, although potatoes also fall into this category. Market characteristics vary drastically. Cocoa, coffee and sugar markets are quite sensitive to the London market. New York orange juice futures are tied almost exclusively to Florida production and a residual of imports. Potato futures prices depend on supplies from specific areas.

Moreover, potatoes are a perishable commodity and must be consumed by the June following the fall harvest. Thus a bull market drives the May contract higher to keep enough potatoes on hand to feed the market during the intervening months. Contrary to potatoes, most tropical product futures behave in a way similar to the grains because they have carryover stocks.

These food futures markets are highly uncertain. Two tongue-in-cheek warnings are worth heeding, if you intend to invest your fortune in these markets: (1) If you can drink it, don't trade it. (2) If you want to trade tropical products, lie down until the feeling subsides. They tend to be higher risk adventures than other commodities. These markets often are thin and in the hands of the "locals." You can be quite correct on your outlook but find it difficult to manage the risk. Cocoa, for instance, has a habit of erupting from a quiet trading range market with no apparent change in the fundamentals.

Coffee, cocoa and orange juice share one common factor: They all are produced from trees. If a crop is decimated by unfavorable weather, drought or frost, the replanting period takes two or more years. Grains can adjust more rapidly from one production season to another.

These markets have been plagued by competition from substitutes. Sugar, for example, now produced largely from beets and tropical cane, faces future price pressure from fructose corn syrup, which can be produced at prices below breakeven for beet and cane sugars. Also, government support prices in the U.S. result in domestic sugar prices that are well above world sugar prices. Substitutes for cocoa butter and powder have trimmed demand since the record highs in 1977.

Aside from potatoes, which are included in the excellent statistical work of the USDA, most food futures rely upon overseas statistical reports, either from London brokerage houses or the producer countries. The latter sources are of dubious value, especially Brazilian crop estimates of coffee or soybeans. African markets for cocoa and coffee are plagued with problems of smuggling and farmer neglect of the crops because of low prices paid to farmers by the government. In several of these markets, attempts by producers cooperating to drive prices higher periodically create artificial price rallies. However, these attempts have not been successful in reversing long-term trends.

In conclusion, the trick to trading tropical products is to be well-funded and be able to pick the long-term trend correctly.

The Metals Group: Buffeted by Monetary Trends

The personalities of the metals futures differ considerably. Each is affected by monetary conditions, but they run the spectrum from a hedge against the dollar to a barometer of the health of the industrial sector in this order: gold, silver, platinum, copper.

The gold market now spans the globe: Zurich, London, New York, Chicago and Hong Kong. This market has become very liquid, and orders can be placed round-the-clock. The monetary role of gold has been de-emphasized by international monetary organizations in recent years, but gold still remains attractive to many as a hedge against paper currencies which are not convertible into any commodity at a fixed rate.

The popularity of owning gold for its own sake rather than for its uses in industry or the high-fashion jewelry trade has grown considerably since U.S. citizens were allowed to legally own gold in 1974 after a 30-year ban. In the Near and Far East, many prefer to store savings in gold rather than savings accounts because of laws on earning interest and the threats of political instability. The risk of gold ownership remains great, however; central banks now possess a 35-year supply. And when inflation subsides and Treasury Bill interest rates turn attractive, investors shift their money from gold and other precious metals to U.S. government instruments.

How much gold exists in the world? Of the three billion ounces or so mined since the dawn of man, most remains in existence and would all fit inside a large barn. Most of the gold is produced in South Africa or the Soviet Union, and its value is affected by the cost of production and by the political situation in the world. Any threats to world stability result in a flurry of gold investment and higher prices.

Who owns the gold? According to recent J. Aron Commodities Corp. figures, world gold stocks of about 2.7 billion oz. are distributed as follows: 10% undetermined or lost; 21% in jewelry, decorative and religious uses; 22% in private hoards or investments; 1% in China; 4% in the USSR; 37% in central banks, and 5% in the Bank for International Settlements and the International Monetary Fund (IMF).

Platinum, like gold, is mined largely in South Africa and the

Soviet Union. The platinum group metals, which include palladium, also traded in futures, are dominated by a few firms. Like
cocoa and coffee, trading the platinum group is a very high risk.

Silver has its price outlook more firmly fixed in industrial usage
although speculative fever can cause some astounding price moves
as in 1980. A third of the silver consumption comes from uses in
photography; should that industry discover a nonsilver catalyst,
silver prices would be affected. Offsetting this threat is the return
to silver coinage by a number of countries. Consumption continues
to outpace production, and over the long term, world stocks have

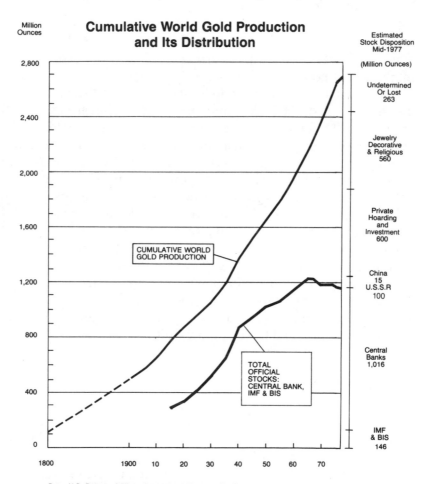

Cumulative World Gold Production and Its Distribution

Data: U.S. Bureau of Mines, International Monetary Fund,
Charter Consolidated, and J. Aron Precious Metals Research Department

Chart prepared by J. Aron Precious Metals Research Department

been declining. Unlike gold, silver is not threatened by large government stocks. However, it is sensitive to a drop in industrial demand due to recession or technological changes.

Copper has a habit of violent price movements out of basing periods. During the last few years, this red metal has come under pressure from developing countries bent on increasing production at any cost in order to acquire foreign exchange. To some extent, copper benefits from a rising gold price. Copper does provide some of the characteristics of a monetary hedge. If gold and silver take off, copper is the next logical bet for a price advance.

The metal markets suffer from some of the statistical problems of the tropical products. Weeks can go by without any important fundamental developments. The level of production of precious metals in the Soviet Union remains in doubt, and selling policies of the Soviets can heavily affect the prices of both gold and platinum. Gold, in particular, remains a political metal subject to the forces at work in dealing with instability in foreign exchange markets.

The Financial Group: Snowballing Growth

Financial instrument futures have grown at an incredible pace since their inception a few years ago. If you include the foreign currency markets as a form of financial instruments, their share of the market is even greater. As long as interest rates and exchange rates continue to roller-coaster, these markets will expand, offering profitable trading opportunities and a bigger need to reduce risk.

Common Mistakes in Fundamental Analysis

Fundamental analysis of commodities is not a complete system but a tool and a framework within which to build the odds of positioning a successful trade. Your odds will improve if you can avoid some common errors made by even seasoned analysts.

The biggest oversight made by traders who are new to futures speculation is to presume that their knowledge of some event or statistic comes as a surprise to the market. Even the best traders have difficulty not wedding themselves to their ideas. Always have a method of testing the waters and timing your trades.

If you do have some news or analysis that you think deserves a position, try to remember the following points in using it:

1. Always compare a news event to the existing price level. The news often is most bullish at the top of the market. When bullish

news fails to push prices higher, it may be time to step aside or go short. "Buy the rumor and sell the fact" is a market axiom that often holds true.

2. Never time your trades based on fundamental information. A method of entry and exit must come from other sources of price analysis.

3. Where possible, use multi-year comparisons. Comparing consumption or production to just one year ago may be misleading. For example, livestock slaughter may be greater than a year ago, but last year's slaughter rates may have been at their lowest level in history.

4. In a highly inflationary environment, all commodity prices tend to rise together. Do not confuse this general rise in prices with cause and effect. Rising grain prices certainly do not always imply rising livestock prices, for example.

5. A producer breakeven price for a commodity is no floor under a market, unless backed by a government support program. Some commodities, such as sugar, can plunge a good deal below that level. Of course, in the long run, a free market will adjust to breakeven levels or better, but in the short run, your trading account may be cleaned out.

6. Consumption is not the same thing as demand. Increasing usage of a commodity, especially perishable products such as meats and potatoes, does not mean increasing demand. High per capita beef consumption may say more about a glut of hamburger than a growth in beef demand. The supply will be consumed at a price. Demand is a function of such slow-changing items as consumer preference, population and income.

7. Be sure that a piece of fundamental news is not in the market already. Some reports are merely summaries of weekly or daily information that is already bid into prices. A monthly gold sale price is a more important figure to the market than the monthly soybean crush statistics which tally weekly usage. This underscores the importance of keeping up on the commodity or commodities you trade.

8. Do not ignore the general economic environment. This last point deserves special consideration.

A fundamental analyst must pay attention to the value of a commodity, both in relation to other commodities and in terms of currency values and domestic inflation rates. The nominal or strict dollar value of a commodity can be deceiving if markets are moving into a period of accelerating inflation or depreciating currency, or contrary wise.

Inflation and currency depreciation have many effects on commodity markets. Those most sensitive will be, of course, the financial instrument futures, foreign currencies and gold. In fact, when the dollar is declining, gold can rise in price during a general selloff in commodities. Under conditions of extreme inflation or deflation, government intervention may seriously distort free market adjustments. A rising inflation rate can stimulate demand as consumers assume they might as well buy now rather than later.

What is the effect of foreign exchange rate fluctuations on commodities? If a currency is appreciating in value because its country has a low inflation rate or a trade surplus, it may be a mixed blessing. For example, a rising Japanese yen makes U.S. cotton cheaper, encouraging exports, but the same rising yen makes Japanese textiles less competitive, reducing the need to import cotton.

The issue of currency changes is beyond the scope of this chapter, but some effects are fairly evident. Trade barriers can influence currency effect. For example, because of levy barriers against feed grains, a depreciating dollar can boost soybean and soybean meal imports to the European Economic Community (EEC). If the dollar is declining, foreign buyers may stand aside from the markets, looking for cheaper prices. This wait-and-see attitude can bunch up buying but may have little or no effect on the level of annual demand. In fact, a chaotic foreign exchange rate structure can precipitate trade controls which are deadly to commodity prices that rely on world trade.

If you accept fundamental supply/demand analysis as part of an overall trading program, it can improve your perspective. Of course, shocks on the system, such as earthquakes, wars, union strikes and embargoes change the game overnight. But these events are rare and, more often than not, fit into the general thrust of a futures price trend. To trade successfully, you must forecast correctly but must not fall in love with your forecast.

8
Analyzing Price Trends: Charts

The minute-by-minute action of fast-changing futures prices is part of the thrill and excitement of trading. But that action is confusing as well. If you watch those tick-by-tick price changes in your broker's office, you can easily lose track of basic price trends. And the big money in futures trading comes from riding the trend, not picking spot trades.

Keep in mind that in the midst of all that excitement, the basic forces of supply and demand are at work. The erratic price changes are simply a function of how all the people who are trading interpret those supply and demand facts. Each person is privy to different information and interpretation. So while you think it's extremely obvious that T-Bonds must rally, there are other traders who believe just the opposite. Both of you are relying on basic fundamental information. But that information may not be the same or the two of you may interpret it differently.

The basic fact to keep in mind: No one trader knows all the facts. Large financial institutions and commercial grain companies obviously have the jump on small investors when it comes to knowlege. They must because that is their living. So how can you compete with their information systems? You can't.

Fortunately, there is a way you can compete, and it's much cheaper than forming a worldwide information network. It's called technical analysis, or charting. Basically, you study the very human reaction to greed and fear as expressed through price action. You compare the way prices are acting now with how they acted in the past. Many times, that same sort of price pattern has developed before. Therefore, you can assume the resulting price action has a very good chance of occurring again. That's because people react to greed and fear in the same way nearly all the time.

Why Charting Works

Charting is an art, not a science. But it can offer clues to future price direction. Reason: Charting depends on prices, and prices are the basic result of supply and demand. It's the only measure you have. All that is known about supply and demand each day is reflected in that day's price. Each day's price reflects everyone's knowledge and opinion of the fundamentals, not just the knowledge and opinion of a few people.

Another reason charts work is because people make them work. The daily price quotes are flashed around the world. These prices are then entered on the price charts of countless traders, from small speculators like yourself to large financial institutions, grain companies, mining companies and central banks. These thousands of people analyze the charts using the same charting rules that have applied for several decades. The result: A very large majority of those thousands of traders reach the same conclusion. They act accordingly, and the charts become self-fulfilling. As a small investor, you're much better off knowing what the big traders think and how they will act. By following their charting techniques, you can join them in their trades.

What Are Charts?

Futures price charts simply record each day's price action for a particular futures and contract. The chart of the June heating oil contract is typical. This chart is a bar chart. It shows prices on the vertical column and trading dates across the bottom. Saturdays and Sundays are left out to help give the chart a continuous picture. Holidays are left blank. The solid bar marked for each day shows that day's trading range by connecting the highest and lowest price paid that day. A small horizontal line is drawn across the solid line to indicate the price at which trading closed that day. This is called the settlement price.

Sometimes you will find dots on the chart instead of a price bar. This happens when all trading for that day occurs at one price. This occurs when prices are "locked up the limit" or "locked down the limit." That means the only trading that occurred was at the set limit from the previous day's settlement as determined by the exchange. Dots can also occur when trading activity is so thin that only a few contracts are traded. This happens in the early days of trading of a new contract.

There are several other types of charts, such as moving average and point-and-figure charts. These are covered in the next chapter. However, the bar chart is by far the most commonly used and is basic to any training on charting.

You've just had the basics of chart construction. You can make your own, based on quotations received over the radio or from your newspaper. However, the easiest method is to buy a chart service. These provide you with already-completed charts, and you usually receive them by Monday morning so you have them in time for the week's trading. You can update them during the week. But you get a clean, updated set every Monday on which you can draw new lines. These services normally sell for $200 to $400 per year, or $4 to $8 per week. You can also receive charts daily or even during the day's trading through the use of your own computer or by subscribing to a special service. These provide a fresh, clean chart whenever you want it.

How You Can Use Charts

Price charts are used to judge probable price direction. It's your ability to judge market thinking and psychology that is the key to charting. The charts reflect human ideas concerning price, given traders' knowledge of supply and demand.

Basic charting techniques help you spot overall price trends — up, down and sideways. There's no secret in making this determination. If the charts shows a succession of lower highs and lower lows, the trend is down. And if there are higher highs and higher lows, the trend is up. Simple. But the real key comes in monitoring the key groups of people who are either in or out of the market and analyze how they might react.

The People in the Market

The price of a particular futures contract is the result of a decision on the part of both a buyer and a seller. The buyer believes prices will go higher; the seller feels prices will decline. These decisions are represented by a trade at an exact price.

Once the buyer and seller make their trade, the influence of their buying and selling in the market is spent — except for the opposite reaction they will ultimately have when they close the trade. Thus, there are two aspects to every trade: 1) Each trade must ultimately have an opposite reaction on the market, and 2) the trade will influence other traders.

Each trader's reaction to price movements can be generalized into the reactions of three basic groups of traders who are always present in the market: 1) Traders who have long positions; 2) traders who have short positions; and 3) those who have not yet taken a position but soon will. Traders in the third group have mixed views on the market's probable direction. Some are bullish while others are bearish, but a lack of positive conviction has kept them out of the market. Therefore, they also have no vested interest in the market's direction.

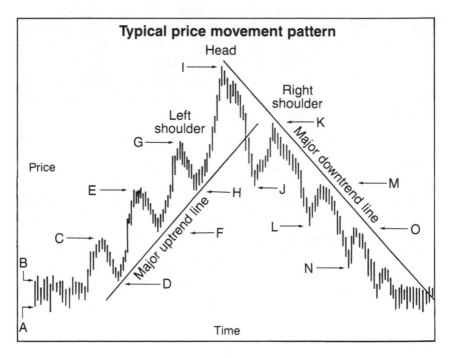

It is this latter group that wields the greatest power since their market impact is still in "reserve." They neither fret nor rejoice as the market moves. But as it moves, their particular market bias is either strengthened or diminished. The most important aspect of the psychology of this group is that they want to go with the market, whichever the direction. They are awaiting a confirmation of their market views. Now look at the typical price pattern from price low to price low to see how this group influences prices. Follow the typical price pattern on the chart on page 94 to see how the psychology expresses itself visually through prices.

The Base Is Built

Assume prices trade within a relatively narrow range as shown in the trading between points A and B on the chart. Recognizing the sideways price movement, the "longs" might buy additional contracts if the price advances above the recent trading range. They may even enter stop orders to buy at B, to add to their position if they should get some confirmation the trend is higher. But by the same token, recognizing prices might decline below the recent trading range and move lower, they might also enter stop orders below the market at A to limit their loss.

The "shorts" have exactly the opposite reaction to the market. Many of them might place stop loss orders above the market at point B to limit losses if the market rallies high enough to shove above point B. But they, too, may add to their position if the price should decline below point A with orders to sell additional contracts on a stop below point A.

The third group is not in the market, but they are watching it for a signal either to go long or short. This group may have stop orders to buy above point B, because presumably the price trend would begin to indicate an upward bias if point B were penetrated. they may also have standing orders to sell below point A for the opposite reasons. As long as prices remain in this sideways pattern, the market is merely forming a base from which it can launch a major rally or decline.

The Uptrend Begins

Assume the market advances to point C. If the trading range between points A and B has been relatively narrow and the time period of the lateral movement relatively long, the accumulated buy stops above the market could be quite numerous. That helps push prices higher on the initial surge above point B. Also, as the market rallies above point B, brokers contact their clients with the news and that results in a stream of new market orders. As this flurry of buyers becomes satisfied and profit-taking from previous long positions (sell orders placed to cancel long positions) causes the market to dip from the high of point C and point D, another distinct attitude begins working in the market.

Part of the first group that went long between points A and B did not buy additional contracts as the market rallied to point C. Now they may be willing to add to their position "on a dip." Consequently, buy orders trickle in from these traders as the market drifts down.

The second group of traders with short positions established in the original trading range but operating without stop loss orders above point B have now seen prices advance to point C, then decline to move back closer to the price at which they originally sold. Since they did not cover their short positions on a buy stop above point B, they may be more than willing to "cover on any further dip" to minimize the loss.

Those not yet in the market will place price orders just below the market with the idea of "getting in on a dip."

The net effect of the rally from A to C is a psychological change in all three groups. The result is a different tone to the market, where some support could be expected from all three groups on dips. (Support on a chart is defined as the place where the buying of a futures contract is sufficient demand to halt a decline in prices.) As this support is strengthened by an increase in market orders and a raising of buy orders, the market once again advances toward point C. Then, as the market gathers momentum and rallies above point C toward point E, the psychology again changes subtly.

The first group of long traders may now have enough profit to pyramid additional contracts with their profits. In any case, as the market advances, their enthusiasm grows and they set their sights on higher price objectives. Psychologically, they have the market advantage.

The original group who sold short between A and B and who have not yet covered are all carrying increasing losses. Their general attitude is negative because they are losing money and confidence. Their hopes fade as their losses mount. Some of this group begin liquidating their short positions either with stops or market orders. Some reverse their position and go long. This all contributes to the uptrend in prices.

The group which has still not entered the market — either because prices never dropped low enough to execute their buy orders or because they had hesitated to see whether the market was actually moving higher — begins to "buy at the market" in their haste to climb aboard the developing uptrend.

Remember that even if a number of traders have not entered the market because of hesitation, their attitude is still bullish. And perhaps they are even kicking themselves for not getting in earlier. As for those who sold out previously-established long positions at a profit only to see the market move still higher, their attitude is still bullish, too. They may also be among those who are looking to buy on the weakness in prices.

So, with each price setback, the market should find the support of: 1) Traders with long positions who are adding to their positions; 2) traders who are short the market and want to buy back their shorts "if the market will only back down some"; and 3) new traders without a position in the market who want to get aboard what they consider a full-fledged bull market.

This rationale results in price action that features one prominent high after another (points E and G and I) and each prominent reactionary low is higher than the previous low (points D, F and H). In a broad sense, it should appear as an upward series of waves of successively higher highs and higher lows as shown by the "major uptrend line."

How Rallies Top Out

But at some point, the psychology again subtly shifts. The first group with long positions and fat profits are no longer willing to add to their positions. In fact, they are looking for a place to "take profits." This eliminates one group of buy orders to support the market on dips.

The second group of battered traders with short positions has finally been worn down to a nub of die-hard shorts who absolutely refuse to cover their short positions. The last group of weak shorts left the market in a final "blow out" at point I. That leaves only the hard-core shorts and they are no longer a supporting element to the market since they are no longer eagerly waiting to buy the market on dips.

The third group of those who never quite get aboard the up-move become unwilling to buy because they feel the greatest part of the upside move has been missed. They consider the risk on the downside too great when compared to the now-limited upside potential. In fact, they may be looking for a place to "short the market and ride it back down."

When the market demonstrates a noticeable lack of support on a dip that "carries too far to be bullish," it is the first signal of a reversal in psychology. The decline from point I to point J is the classic example of such a dip. This decline signals a new tone to the market. The support on dips becomes resistance on rallies, and a more two-sided market action develops. (Resistance is the opposite of support. Resistance on a chart is the price level where selling pressure is expected to stop advances and possibly turn prices lower.)

How the Downtrend Begins

Now the picture has changed. As the market begins to advance from point J to point K, traders with previously-established long positions take profits by selling out. Most of the hard-nosed traders with short positions have covered their shorts, so they add no significant new buying impetus to the market. In fact, having witnessed the recent long decline, they may be adding to their short positions, bringing more selling pressure into the market.

If the rally back toward the contract highs fails to establish new highs, this failure is quickly noticed by professional traders as a signal the bull market has run its course. This is even more true if the rally carries only up to the approximate level of the rally top at point G.

If the open interest also declines during the rally from J to K, it is another sign it was not new buying that caused the rally but short covering. This is how head-and-shoulders top formations develop, which we will cover later.

As profit-taking and new short-selling forces the market to decline from point K, the next critical point is the reactionary low point at J. A major bear signal is flashed if the market penetrates this prominent low (support) following an abortive attempt to establish new contract highs.

This completes the formation of a head-and-shoulders top. But rather than simply explain away price patterns with names, it is important to understand how the psychology of the market action at different points causes the market to respond as it does. It also explains why certain points are quite significant.

In a bear market, the attitudes of the traders would be reversed.

Each decline would find the bears more confident and prosperous and the bulls more depressed and threadbare. Each correction finds the bears willing sellers as they add to their winning positions. Meanwhile, the bulls anxiously sell out of their losing position on each reaction upward. That limits the advance and keeps the downtrend rolling. With the psychology diametrically opposite, the pattern completely reverses itself to form a series of lower highs (points K, M and O) and lower lows (points L and N).

But at some point, the bears become unwilling to add to their previously-established short positions. Those who were already long the market and had refused to sell higher would eventually be reduced to a hard core of traders who had their jaws set and refused to sell out. Traders not in the market who were perhaps unsuccessfully attempting to short the market at higher levels will begin to find the long side of the market more attractive. The first rally that "carries too high to be bearish" signals another possible trend reversal.

With this basic understanding of market psychology through three phases of a market, a trader is better equipped to appreciate the significance of all technical price patterns. No one expects to establish short positions at the high or long positions at the low, but development of a feel for market psychology is the beginning of the quest for trades that even hindsight could not improve upon. Let's look more closely at specific chart patterns. Although all these examples are from daily charts, the rules work just as well on longer-term charts. Because the longer-term charts cover more time, their trendlines are more important in identifying areas of support and resistance to the market.

Make the Trend Your Friend

"The trend is your friend" is an important trading guideline. Because trends persist for long periods, a position taken with the trend will more likely be successful than one taken randomly or against the trend. Trading with the trend in a bull market means buying on dips; in a bear market, selling on rallies.

A trend is easily spotted on a bar chart. An uptrend is a series of higher lows and higher highs. Uptrend lines are drawn under the lows of the market and give support. A downtrend is a series of lower lows and lower highs. Downtrend lines are drawn across the highs and give resistance to the market. The soybean chart shown

here has both uptrend lines and a downtrend line.

A trendline can be drawn when two points are available. The more times a trendline is touched, the more technically significant this support or resistance line becomes.

While some chartists draw trendlines through lows and highs, others may prefer drawing lines through closes in hopes of detecting a change in trend more quickly.

Trendlines may change angles, requiring another line drawn through new high or low points. For example, the sideways trading action in March and April broke the steeper uptrend line connecting the Feb. 13 and Mar. 20 lows. But when the uptrend resumed in early May, a more shallow uptrend line can be drawn connecting the February and late-April lows.

The most reliable trendlines are those near a 45° angle. If about four weeks have elapsed between the two connecting points, this increases the trendline's validity. However, steep trendlines that don't fit these guidelines, like the uptrend line in the early portion of the soybean chart, may be just as useful.

Often, minor uptrends or downtrends will confuse the beginner. It may seem the market has turned around. However, sharp chartists will see these minor trends as small ripples within a major wave. Remember, if the trendline isn't broken, that trend remains intact.

Two closes outside the trendline are the criteria for detecting a change in trend. However, very seldom do markets go directly from uptrend to downtrend. At the end of a move, traders become less aggressive and prices may swing in a sideways pattern or consolidation period.

Many times, markets break into an uptrend or downtrend out of a sideways trading pattern or consolidation period. In the soybean chart, prices traded in a 50¢ range for nine weeks before breaking the resistance level and beginning a short move up. As a general rule, the longer the consolidation period, the greater the rally after the breakout.

Because traders need time to be convinced they should put their money into the market, sideways patterns are more likely to occur near the bottom of a move. The beginning of a downtrend often will be sharp and sudden as investors pull money out of the market.

Another way beginners might be fooled is seeing false breakouts of tops and bottoms. As prices begin to make their move in switching from a downtrend to an uptrend, traders with short positions will "cover." This buying many times will cause the market to rally above the downtrend line. This short-covering rally seldom holds, and prices may drop back to the breakout point. The uptrend is confirmed when prices close above the high of the short rally.

On a topping formation, long liquidation takes prices through the uptrend line on a short break. Before the downtrend begins, the market sometimes rallies back to "test" the uptrend line as shown on the soybean chart in September. As the downtrend unfolds, the second reaction rally could not top the highs of the first rally.

Channel lines are an extension of the trendline theory. The October through January downtrend on the soybean chart shows prices staying in a "channel" between the downtrend line and a line drawn parallel to it, connecting the lows. A channel line in a downtrending market helps identify where support may be found.

Speedlines Highlight Key Trends, Too

Speedlines are another tool which show where prices may find support or resistance. Frequently, speedlines and trendlines will overlap, emphasizing that line's importance to the market.

The speedline on the soybean chart starts from the June 29 low. To find the points to connect with the low, divide the range between the low ($6.40) and the high ($9.94) into thirds and subtract that amount from the high.

Plot the point obtained by subtracting one-third of the range from the high on the day the high was made. A line drawn between this point ($8.76) and the low established the 1/3 speedline. The 2/3 speedline is drawn through the point that is two-thirds of the range subtracted from the high ($7.58) plotted on the day the high was made.

How Gaps Measure Market Moves

Gaps are one of the most easily recognizable technical indicators. A gap is simply an empty spot formed on a chart when price lines don't overlap the previous day's price action. Sometimes market psychology changes overnight or over a weekend. That change in psychology forces prices to open and stay above or below the previous day's range.

"Gaps are filled" is another time-tested rule of the market. That is why gaps become future price objectives. Quite often, prices retreat to fill a gap in a bull market before continuing the move. Likewise, prices often rally in a bear market to fill gaps.

Gaps may serve one of three purposes. They are used to spot the beginning of a move, to measure a move and to signal the end. There are four different kinds of gaps: common or temporary, breakaway, measuring or runaway, and exhaustion.

The most frequently occurring gap is the common gap. When this gap occurs because of a slight change in psychology, traders expect it to be filled soon. Once a gap is filled, it no longer has significance.

The early portion of the soybean chart on page 103 shows common gaps during the December and January period which were later filled.

The breakaway gap on this chart occurred on May 7 and begins a major bull move. Breakaway gaps often occur after a stretch of sideways trading and in the leading days of an uptrend or downtrend. This type of gap remains unfilled for a long time.

Sometimes it is difficult to determine right away that a gap is a breakaway gap and not a common gap. When the market fails to fill

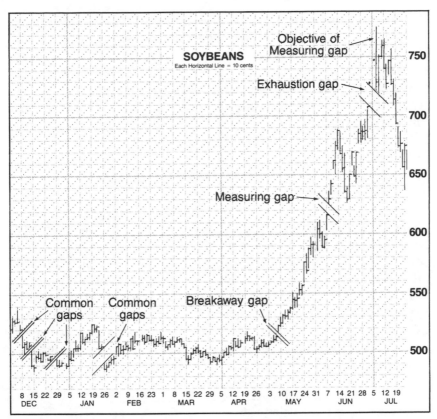

Objective of
Measuring gap

SOYBEANS
Each Horizontal Line = 10 cents

Exhaustion gap

Measuring gap

Common
gaps

Common
gaps

Breakaway gap

750

700

650

600

550

500

8 15 22 29 5 12 19 26 2 9 16 23 1 8 15 22 29 5 12 19 26 3 10 17 24 31 7 14 21 28 5 12 19
DEC   JAN   FEB   MAR   APR   MAY   JUN   JUL

this gap after a couple weeks, it confirms the breakaway gap.

A measuring gap typically occurs in the middle of a price move and predicts how much farther the move will go. It is also called a midpoint gap and a runaway gap.

On this soybean chart, the measuring gap, which occurred on June 8, left an empty spot from $6.16 to $6.26. The April 5 low at $4.90 marked the beginning of this move. The distance from the low at $4.90 to the measuring gap is $1.26 to $1.36. Adding this distance to the measuring gap projects a move to at least $7.50. Whether you add the distance to the top, bottom or middle of the measuring gap depends on your preference.

An exhaustion gap shows frustrated bears giving up and aggressive bulls trying to make the market go their way. It is the first sign of sputtering before the end.

Though prices may go higher after an exhaustion gap at the top, the rally will not last long before the market dies. An extreme exhaustion gap may form an island reversal.

What about gaps that remain unfilled? They become future chart objectives. If gaps are unfilled when a futures contract expires, there are usually corresponding gaps on the charts of subsequent contract months.

Gaps also appear on longer-term charts such as weekly commodity charts, but gaps on monthly charts are rare because they generally are constructed to avoid gaps caused by contract changeover. Like those on the daily charts, gaps on weekly charts are also "made to be filled".

How Key Reversals Signal Changes

One of the most easily recognizable technical signals in trend change is the key reversal. A key reversal often has an unusually wide trading range. Its requirements are a day's range outside the previous day's range with a close higher than the previous close for an upward turnaround and a lower close for a downward turn.

Here again, this chart formation reflects market psychology. A key reversal is the climax of a period of buying or selling fever. In extremely volatile markets, two or more key reversals may occur. The key reversal on the silver chart defined the top of its rally and signaled a fall in prices.

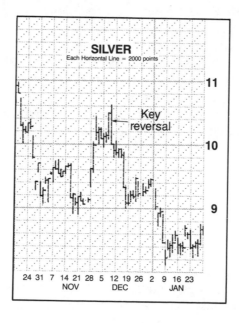

To be a valid key reversal top, trading volume must be heavy and the daily trading range should be wide. Prices first surge to new highs, but fall back and close lower for the day.

For a key reversal bottom, the characteristics are the same. The selling climax has to have heavy volume with a wide trading range which first breaks to new lows, rebounds above the previous day's high and closes higher. Frequently, the highest trading volume and the highest or lowest price of the year will be set on a key reversal day.

An island reversal takes gaps to the extreme. It receives its name for obvious reasons. An island reversal can be only one day or a few days of trading above (or below) the previous and following days' trading activity. The action is isolated by gaps on both sides. Thus, it leaves a day or a few days of price action surrounded by empty space.

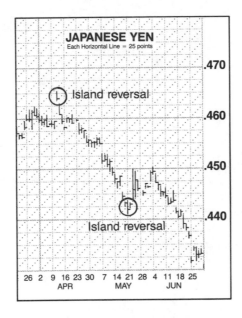

The Japanese yen chart shows two island reversals. The 1-day island top of April 11 marked the climax of a bull move and the beginning of falling prices. The 3-day island reversal bottom in mid-May signalled a halt to the decline and the beginning of a bear market rally. However, the downtrend eventually resumed, plunging prices under the island reversal.

Island reversals occur less frequently than key reversals. The exhaustion gap which marks the beginning of the island reversal will remain unfilled for a lengthy period because the island reversal is usually the climax to an existing trend.

Strong Signals in Double Bottoms and Tops

One way to detect a change in trend is by looking for a price from which the market reacts two or three times.

A double bottom, such as the one on the T-Bill chart, indicated the 87.10 to 87.20 area gave support to the market. Although a recovery had begun from the late-May low, prices broke the short-term uptrend in mid-June. The question then became: Will aggressive short-selling and long liquidation overwhelm the short-covering and new buying that come from support at the May low?

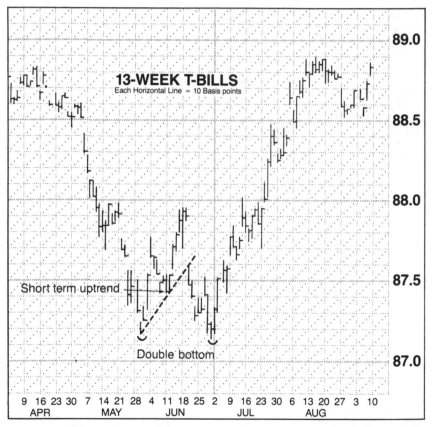

The soybean chart on page 100 displays a triple top, where prices met resistance in approximately the same area three times before falling. Just the inverse of making the double bottom goes through traders' minds as the market makes a top: Will new buying and short-covering be able to overwhelm the new selling and long liquidation coming from the triple-top resistance area?

As with trendlines, the more time that elapses between the tests of support and resistance in double or triple tops or bottoms, the more valid the formation becomes. Also, the greater the reaction between tests of the support or resistance, the more likely the point will hold.

A "V" bottom can develop as well, when prices plunge to a new low and then quickly recover. More thinly-traded, but heavily-trend-oriented, markets such as currencies and livestock are noted for their "V" bottoms.

Saucer Bottoms: The Darkness Before Dawn

A downtrend may slide to a slow, gradual halt in the saucer bottom formation. Open interest and volume follow the same pattern as prices in this formation, reflecting speculator disinterest in a market with little action and little profit potential. Our example on the monthly cocoa chart took three years to form. Saucer bottoms on daily charts may take at least four weeks to become visible.

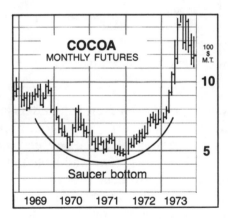

Although this bottom formation doesn't meet the requirements of other bottom formations, it's just as significant in signaling a trend change. Usually, the longer it takes to form a saucer bottom, the more violently prices will rise out of their lows.

Head-and-Shoulders Bottom: Old Reliable

When prices form pictures on charts, you can obtain realistic objectives for later moves. One of the most reliable chart formations is the head-and-shoulders top or bottom. This easily recognizable chart pattern is seen in the accompanying weekly gold chart and signals a major turn in trend.

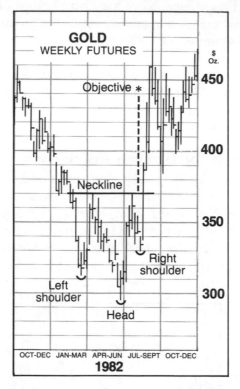

The main advantage of the head-and-shoulders pattern is it gives you a clear-cut objective of the price move after breaking out of the formation. Measure the price distance between the head and the neckline, which is $75 in this case, and add it to the price where the neckline is broken. This projects the minimum objective. Although the head-and-shoulders formation gives no time projection, it predicts gold eventually would move to $445.

In most cases, a head-and-shoulders formation will be symmetrical, with the left and right shoulders equally developed. Although the neckline doesn't have to be horizontal, the most reliable formations stray only a little.

Flags, Pennants, Coils Point the Way

Flags and pennants are consolidation patterns which give objectives for further moves. As the formation develops, price action in an uptrending market will look like a flag flying from a flagpole as prices tend to form a parallelogram after a quick, steep upmove. Flags "fly at half-mast." The more vertical the flagpole, the better.

A price objective is obtained by measuring the flagpole and adding it to the breakout point of the formation, as shown on corn's weekly chart. The flagpole should begin at the point from which it broke away from a previous congestion area, or from important support or resistance lines. Flags in a downtrending market look like they are defying gravity and slant upward.

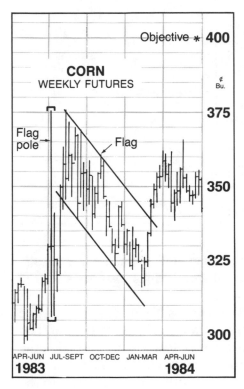

A pennant also starts with a nearly vertical price rise or fall. But, instead of having equal-move reactions in the consolidation phase like a flag, pennant reactions gradually decrease to form short uptrend and downtrend lines from the flagpole.

The same measuring tools used in flags are used in pennants. Add the length of the flagpole to the breakout point to get the

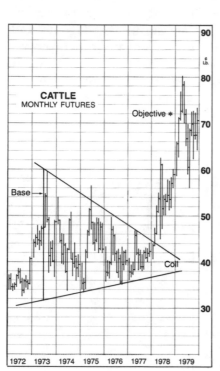

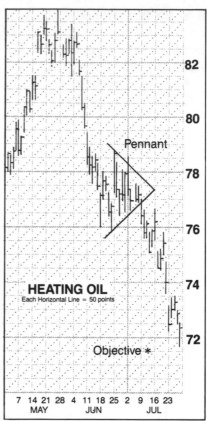

minimum objective. Remember, flags and pennants are usually continuation patterns in an overall trend which resumes after the breakout of the consolidation area.

Also, the coil formation, or symmetrical triangle, appears while prices trade in continually narrower ranges, forming uptrend and downtrend lines. This pattern doesn't tell you much about the direction of the next move. After breaking one of the trendlines, the objective is found by adding the width of the coil's base to the breakout point.

The formation gets its name from the way prices contract and suddenly spring out of this pattern like a tight coil spring. One caution about this formation: It's best if prices break out of the formation while halfway to three-quarters of the way to the triangle's apex. If prices reach the apex, a strong move in either direction is less likely.

Triangles Yield Objectives, Too

Ascending and descending triangles are similar to coils but are much better at predicting the direction prices will take. Prices should break to the flat side of the triangle.

Price objectives from ascending and descending triangles can be obtained two ways. The easiest is to add the length of the left side of the triangle to the triangle's flat side.

Another method of projecting price is to draw a line parallel to the sloping line from the beginning of the triangle. Expect prices to rise or fall out of the triangle formation until they reach this parallel line.

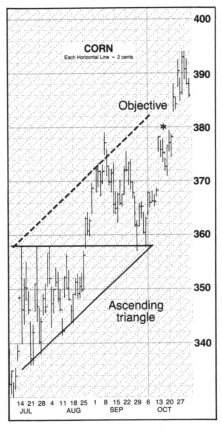

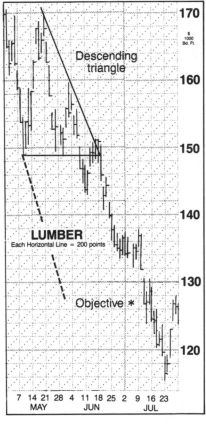

9
Analyzing Price Trends: Moving Averages, Point-and-Figure, RSI and Others

Besides simple technical analysis based on the study of bar charts, many futures traders also look for an objective trading system that will flash trading signals. With the advent of computers, this process has exploded in recent years. In this chapter, we will cover the basics of a few, key systems.

Trading the Trend with Moving Averages

Moving averages are one tool to help you detect a change in trend. They measure buying and selling pressures under the assumption that no commodity can sustain an uptrend or downtrend without consistent buying and selling pressure.

A moving average is an average of a number of consecutive prices updated as new prices become available. The moving average swallows temporary price aberrations but tells you when prices begin moving consistently in one direction.

Trading with moving averages will never position you in the market at precisely the right time. They are intended to help you take profits from the middle of the trend and hold losses to a minimum.

The risks and the magnitude are intrinsic to the speed of the moving averages. Professional traders lean toward the faster averages and portfolio managers generally prefer slower signaling moving average approaches.

Moving averages are a simple way to gauge the direction the tide is flowing in a commodity market. They are not always right, but they provide a wide variety of possible uses.

Moving averages lag prices because of their makeup. You can make a moving average for any number of days you choose, but remember that the more days you average, the more sluggish the moving average becomes. Most commodity traders find a 3-day moving average alone is too volatile. However, 4-day and 5-day moving averages are common as short-term indicators.

To start a 4-day moving average, add the last four days' closing prices and divide by four. The next day, drop off the oldest price, add the new close, and divide by four again. The result is the new moving average. Use the same system for any moving average you might want to develop.

Moving averages give signals when different averages cross one another. For example, in using 4-day, 9-day and 18-day moving averages, a buy signal would be given when the 9-day average crosses the 18-day. However, to avoid false signals, the 4-day average should be higher than the 9-day.

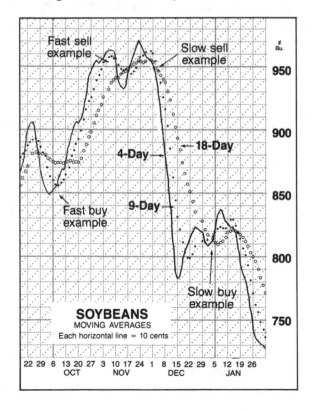

Just the opposite is true for sell signals. To sell, the 4-day average must be below the 9-day. The sell signal is triggered when the 9-day average crosses the 18-day.

There are other conditions you might wish to place on your averages to avoid false signals. One possible requirement is to make the 4-day exceed the 9-day by a certain percentage before acting on the appropriate buy or sell signal.

The caveat to moving averages is that although they work well in trending markets, they may whipsaw you in a sideways, choppy market. Such was the case during the sideways trading periods of the soybean chart shown here.

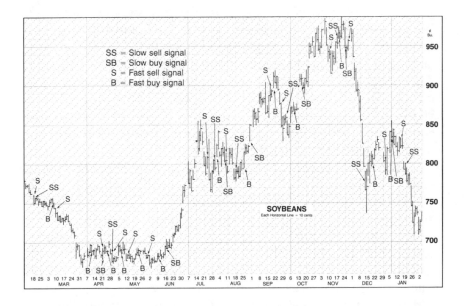

By strictly following the conditions laid out here, which closed out a position and took a new one at the day's close following the signal, the slower moving averages gained a total from all trades of $3.38¼, but lost $3.45¼ from all trades by Jan. 16. That's a 7¢ loss plus about $750 for 15 commissions for a total expense of $1,100.

Taking signals using just the 4-day and 9-day averages did a little better. That would have gained $4.65¼ and lost $4.49½ from the beginning of the contract for all trades. The 15¾¢ profit did not cover the $1,450 cost of the 29 commissions, creating a loss of $662.50.

Therefore, a bit of brainwork is necessary to use a moving average. The slower moving average's strong point was that it caught the early downtrend and most of the summer upmove to gain $1.62 (before commissions) by the time it got you short on July 30.

The market then turned sideways and the moving averages gave signals at the end of reactions. If you had blindly followed those signals, you would have lost $1.03¾ plus the cost of 9 commissions between July 30 and Dec. 4.

Some traders who use moving averages follow the slower moving average signals to initiate a position but a faster moving average to exit the trade, especially if substantial profits have been built up.

Assume you had gone long with the buy signal on June 17. Within a month, you had gained about $1.50 and prices started falling. If you decided to use the faster 4-day/9-day signal that came on July 23, you would have gotten out of your long position the next day when prices ranged between $8.30 and $7.80. The slower signal on July 30 would have gotten you out July 31 between $8.25 and $8.10. In this particular case, both the faster and slower averages got you out of your long position at nearly the same price. But this wasn't the case in later trading activity.

Neither method worked well in the congestion phase that lasted until late August. However, a faster signal would have gotten you into the next upmove 40¢ to 50¢ better than the slower signal. It also would have gotten you out of the position about 50¢ better.

After the climb into late September, once again, both methods placed you badly during the reaction. But, from late October, the moving average chart shows how you can watch the faster averages when profits might reach the "windfall" stage.

Although the faster signal didn't do well on its first two signals, it did give a sell signal five days and about 80¢ earlier than the slower signal before the December crash.

A linearly-weighted moving average also could help eliminate false signals. A 4-day linearly-weighted moving average multiplies the oldest price by four, the next oldest price by three, etc., and divides the total by 10.

This weighted average is more sensitive to recent prices than a standard average. The term, "linearly-weighted," comes from the fact that each day's contribution diminishes by one digit.

The rules for trading a weighted moving average are the same as using a combination of three moving averages. The weighted average must be above or below the other moving averages, or the signal is ignored.

A more sophisticated average is the exponential moving average, which is weighted nonlinearly by using a specific smoothing constant derived for each commodity to allocate the weight exponentially back over prior trading days.

However, it requires high mathematics and a computer to determine each optimum smoothing constant.

Point-and-Figure Charts Give Specific Signals

Their appearance may be deceiving since they look like an elongated version of tic-tac-toe. Yet, point-and-figure charts provide another means of determining a trend. In fact, their advantage over a bar chart is the specific buy and sell signals — no personal interpretation is needed.

The pork belly chart is shown for the same time period in both bar chart and point-and-figure form. The differences in appearance are striking. This is due mainly to the lack of a time scale on the point-and-figure chart. Time is irrelevant; price movements are charted only when they occur. On days when no new high or low is made, no additional entries are made on the chart.

Also, on a point-and-figure chart, the price scale marks the space between the lines rather than on the lines as bar charts are marked.

Upward price action in a point-and-figure chart is indicated by X's; downward movement by O's.

The point-and-figure chart gives a simple buy signal when an X in the latest column has filled a box that is one box higher than the preceding column of X's. A simple sell signal appears when the latest column is in O's, and the O's fill the box below the previous column of O's. These simple signals are marked on the pork belly point-and-figure chart on the next page.

Each point-and-figure chart you see will have a box size and reversal number. In this case, it is 40 × 6, which means each box is worth 40 points, and it takes a price change of six full boxes in the opposite direction to start a new column. When beginning a new column, the box adjacent to the last entry is always left empty.

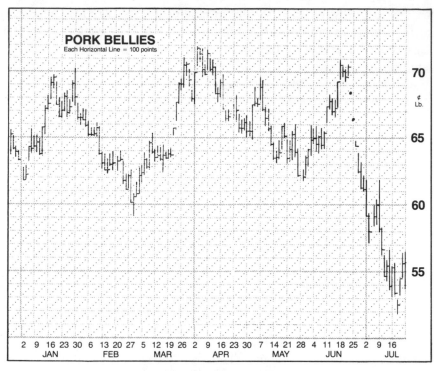

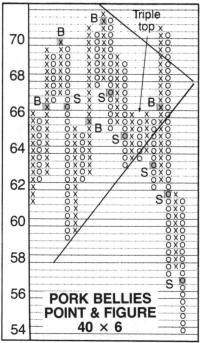

Rules for Plotting

When plotting X's, wait for the price to rise to fill the entire box before adding another X to the current column. Likewise, when working with a downtrending column of O's, wait for prices to drop to fill the whole box before adding another O to the column. Based on a single day's price action, you don't add to the current column and then plot a reversal. If you continued the current column of X's or O's, don't start a new column based on one day's price action.

For example, if the most recent column is X's, look at the daily high first. If the high is high enough to require drawing one or more

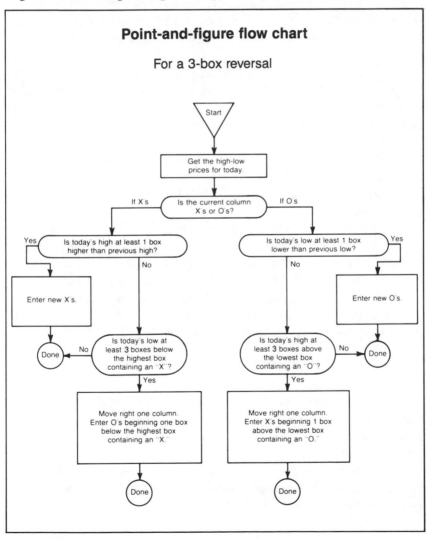

additional X's in the current column, the daily low is ignored, regardless of how low it might be. If the trend has truly reversed, it will be revealed the following day. *Only* if you can't add an X do you check the low to see if you can fill the required number of boxes for a reversal.

A similar procedure is used when the current column is O's. Look at the daily low first and ignore the high if you can add to the O column. As before, *only* if you can't add an O do you check the high to determine if you can add enough X's for a reversal. A flow chart for plotting a 3-box reversal chart is shown on page 119.

Each vertical column will always have at least the number of X's or O's needed for a reversal. For example, the pork belly illustration of a 40 × 6 box size and reversal will always have at least six X's or O's in each column.

There are many formations on point-and-figure charts, but breakouts of double or triple tops or bottoms are probably the most reliable ones. The last rally (the June rally) on the pork belly point-and-figure chart to just over the 70¢ level was a breakout of a triple top.

Trendlines can also be used on point-and-figure charts. Most traders agree that the 45-degree trendline, which cuts each box diagonally, is more useful than connecting highs or lows as you do on a bar chart.

An uptrend line is started at the lower right hand corner of the box with an O and drawn up to the right at a 45-degree angle. A downtrend line begins at the upper right hand corner of a box with an X and is drawn down at a 45-degree angle to the right.

Breakouts of point-and-figure formations must completely clear the 45-degree line, and, if applicable, move one box higher or lower than the previous column of like letters.

Use Point-and-Figure Selectively

The disadvantage of point-and-figure charts is that they may be slow to signal trend changes. Since point-and-figure traders are buying and selling breakouts, followthrough is needed for a profitable trade. Similar to moving averages, they don't work well in sideways markets.

One way to use the point-and-figure selectively is to ignore minor trend reversals when a new column is started. Some whipsaws may be reduced by ignoring minor signals unless they are in tune with the major trendline on the point-and-figure chart. The charts below show advanced trading signals you can get from point-and-figure charts.

Oscillators Measure Trend Strength

One of the most useful tools employed by many technical commodity traders is a momentum oscillator which measures the ve-

Advanced point-and-figure signals

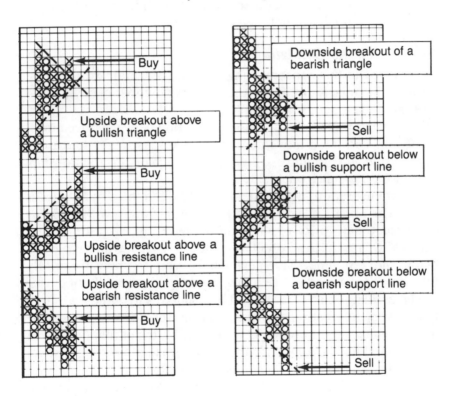

locity of directional price movement.

When prices move up very rapidly, at some point the commodity is considered overbought; when they move down very rapidly, the commodity is considered oversold at some point. In either case, a reaction or reversal is imminent. The slope of the momentum oscillator is directly proportional to the velocity of the move, and the distance traveled up or down by this oscillator is proportional to the magnitude of the move.

The momentum oscillator is usually characterized by a line on a chart drawn in two dimensions. The vertical axis represents magnitude or distance the indicator moves; the horizontal axis represents time. Such a momentum oscillator moves very rapidly at market turning points and then tends to slow down as the market continues the directional move.

Suppose we are using closing prices to calculate the oscillator and the price is moving up daily by exactly the same increment from close to close. At some point, the oscillator begins to flatten out and eventually becomes a horizontal line. If the price begins to level out, the oscillator will begin to descend.

How to Plot the Oscillator

Let's look at this concept using a simple oscillator expressed in terms of the price today minus the price "x" number of days ago — let's say 10 days ago, for example.

The easiest way to illustrate the interaction between price movement and oscillator movement is to take a straight line price relationship and plot the oscillator points used on this relationship, as shown on the chart at right.

In our illustration, we begin on Day 10 when the closing price is 48.50. The price 10 days ago on Day 1 is 50.75. So with a 10-day oscillator, today's price of 48.50 subtracted from the price 10 days ago of 50.75 results in an oscillator value of -2.25, which is plotted below the zero line. The negative is used to show trend. By following this procedure each day, we develop an oscillator curve.

The oscillator curve developed by using this hypothetical situation is very interesting. As the price moves down by the same increment each day between Days 10 and 14, the oscillator curve is a horizontal line. On Day 15, the price turns up by 25 points, yet the oscillator turns up by 50 points. The oscillator is going up twice as fast as the price. The oscillator continues this rate of movement until Day 23 when its value becomes constant, although the price continues to move up at the same rate.

On Day 29, another very interesting thing happens. The price levels out at 51.00, yet the oscillator begins to go down. If the price continues to move horizontally, the oscillator will continue to descend until the 10th day, at which time both the oscillator and the price will be moving horizontally.

Note the interaction of the oscillator curve and the price curve.

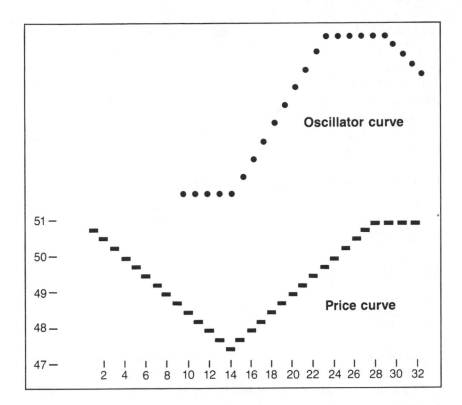

The oscillator appears to be one step ahead of the price. That's because the oscillator, in effect, is measuring the rate of change of price movement. Between Days 14 and 23, the oscillator shows the rate of price change is very fast because the direction of the price is changing from down to up. Once the price has bottomed out and started up, the rate of change slows down because the increments of change are measured in one direction only.

Three Problems with Oscillators

The oscillator can be an excellent technical tool for the trader who understands its inherent characteristics. However, there are three problems encountered in developing a meaningful oscillator:

1. Erratic movement within the general oscillator configuration. Suppose that 10 days ago the price moved limit down from the previous day. Now, suppose that today the price closed the same as yesterday. When you subtract the price 10 days ago from today's price, you will get an erroneously high value for the oscillator today. To overcome this, there must be some way to dampen or

smooth out the extreme points used to calculate the oscillator.

2. The second problem with oscillators is the scale to use on the horizontal axis. How high is high, and how low is low? The scale will change with each commodity. To overcome this problem, there must be some common denominator to apply to all commodities so the amplitude of the oscillator is relative and meaningful.

3. Calculating enormous amounts of data. This is the least of the three problems.

How to Calculate Relative Strength Index

A solution to the three problems associated with oscillators is incorporated in the indicator which we call the Relative Strength Index (RSI):

$$RSI = 100 - \frac{100}{1 + RS}$$

$$RS = \frac{\text{Average of 14 day's closes UP}}{\text{Average of 14 day's closes DOWN}}$$

For the first calculation of the Relative Strength Index (RSI), we need closing prices for the previous 14 days. From then on, we need only the data from the previous day. The initial RSI is calculated as follows:

1. Obtain the sum of the UP closes for the previous 14 days and divide this sum by 14. This is the average UP close.

2. Obtain the sum of the DOWN closes for the previous 14 days and divide this sum by 14. This is the average DOWN close.

3. Divide the average UP close by the average DOWN close. This is the Relative Strength (RS).

4. Add 1.00 to the RS.

5. Divide the result obtained in Step 4 into 100.

6. Subtract the result obtained in Step 5 from 100. This is the first RSI.

From this point on, it is necessary to use only the previous average UP close and the previous average DOWN close in calculating the next RSI. This procedure incorporates the dampening or smoothing factor into the equation:

1. To obtain the next average UP close, multiply the previous average UP close by 13, add to this amount today's UP close (if any) and divide the total by 14.

2. To obtain the next average DOWN close, multiply the previous average DOWN close by 13, add to this amount today's DOWN close (if any) and divide the total by 14.

Steps 3 to 6 are the same as for the initial RSI.

The RSI approach surmounts the three basic problems of oscillators:

1. Erroneous erratic movement is eliminated by the averaging technique. However, the RSI is amply responsive to price movement because an increase of the average UP close is automatically coordinated with a decrease in the average DOWN close and vice versa.

2. The question, "How high is high and how low is low?" is answered because the RSI value must always fall between 0 and 100. Therefore, the daily momentum of any number of commodities can be measured on the same scale for comparison to each other and to previous highs and lows within the same commodity.

3. The problem of having to keep up with mountains of previous data is also solved. After calculating the initial RSI, only the previous day's data is required for the next calculation.

The Relative Strength Index, used in conjunction with a bar chart, can provide a new dimension of interpretation for the chart reader. No single tool, method, or system is going to produce the right answers 100% of the time. However, the RSI can be a valuable input into this decision-making process.

Commodity Price Charts plots the 14-day RSI, updating the chart through Thursday of each week. Contrary to popular opinion, the choice of the number of market days used in calculating the RSI doesn't really matter because the smoothing nature of the exponential averages reduces the effect of the early days as more data is included.

A Simplified RSI Formula

The procedure outlined earlier for beginning and updating RSIs is from J. Welles Wilder's book and his 1978 *Futures* Magazine story, which made the RSI a popular technical tool. The following is a simpler and faster method of computing the RSI. The results are the same as Wilder's more complicated method.

To begin a new RSI, just list the changes for 14 consecutive trading days and total the changes. Divide these totals by 14, and you will have the new up and down average. Then proceed with this formula:

$$RSI = 100 \times \frac{U}{U + D}$$

U = up average; D = down average.

The example below is for T-bills.

Date	Up	Down
1/28	+41	
1/29		−2
2/1		−60
2/2		−7
2/3	+2	
2/4	+1	
2/5	+6	
2/8		−26
2/9	+11	
2/10	+14	
2/11	0	0
2/12		−11
2/16	+28	
2/17		−18
Total	103	124

1.03 ÷ 14 = .074 = Up ave.
1.24 ÷ 14 = .089 = Down ave.

$$RSI = 100 \times \frac{.074}{.163} = 45.39$$

To calculate the next day's RSI, multiply the up average (.074) by 13. Add the change for the day, if it is up. Divide the total by 14. Do the same for the new down average. Multiply the new down average (.089) by 13. Add the change for the day, if it is down. Divide this total by 14.

Then, proceed with the formula:

$$RSI = 100 \times \frac{U}{U + D}$$

For example, if T-Bills closed up 25 points the next day, calculate the new RSI as follows:

New Up ave. $= \dfrac{.074(13) + .25}{14} = .087$

New Down ave. $= \dfrac{.089(13) + 0}{14} = .083$

New RSI $= 100 \times \dfrac{.112}{.112 + .083}$

RSI $= 51.2$

Learning to use this index is a lot like learning to read a chart. The more you study the interaction between chart movement and the Relative Strength Index, the more revealing the RSI will become. If used properly, the RSI can be a very valuable tool in interpreting chart movement.

How to Use RSI

RSI points are plotted daily on a bar chart and, when connected, form the RSI line. Here are some things the index indicates as shown by examples from the silver chart:

Tops and bottoms — These are often indicated when the index goes above 70 or below 30. The index will usually top out or bottom out before the actual market top or bottom, giving an indication a reversal or at least a significant reaction is imminent.

The major bottom of Aug. 15 was accompanied by an RSI value below 30. The major top of Nov. 9 was preceded by an RSI value above 70. The top made on Jan. 24 was preceded by an RSI value of less than 70. This would indicate this top is less significant than the previous one and either a higher top is in the making or the long-term uptrend is running out of steam.

Chart formations — The index will display graphic chart formations which may not be obvious on a corresponding bar chart. For instance, head-and-shoulders tops or bottoms, pennants or triangles often show up on the index to indicate breakouts and buy and sell points.

A descending triangle was formed on the RSI chart during October and early November that is not evident on the bar chart. A breakout of this triangle indicates an intermediate move in the direction of the breakout. Note also the long-term coil on the RSI chart with the large number of support points.

Failure swings — Failure swings above 70 or below 30 (illustrated in Fig. 8 and 9) are very strong indications of a market reversal.

After the RSI exceeded 70 during October, the immediate downswing carried to 65. When this low point of 65 was penetrated the following week, the failure swing was completed.

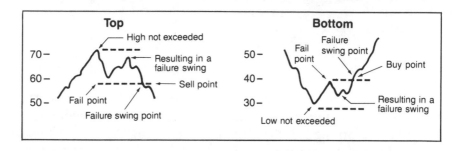

After the low of Aug. 15, the RSI shot up to 41. After two downswings, this point was penetrated on the upside on Aug. 26, completing the failure swing.

Support and resistance — Areas of support and resistance often show up clearly on the index before becoming apparent on the bar chart.

Trendlines on the bar chart often show up as support lines on the RSI. The mid-November break penetrated the uptrend line on the bar chart at the same time as the support level on the RSI chart.

Divergence — Divergence between price action and the RSI is a very strong indicator of a market turning point and is the single most indicative characteristic of the Relative Strength Index. Divergence occurs when the RSI is increasing and price movement is either flat or decreasing. Conversely, divergence occurs when the RSI is decreasing and price movement is either flat or increasing. Divergence does not occur at every turning point.

On the silver chart, there was divergence between the bar chart and RSI at every major turning point. The top made in November was "warned" by the RSI exceeding 70, a failure swing and divergence with the RSI turning sideways while prices continued to climb higher.

Computer Explosion Yields More

The personal computer explosion, along with the development of data bases, resulted in the formation of many new oscillators and computer-generated systems at the time of the writing of this book. The number is too few to cover and each is too complex to summarize in a brief portion of a book. Some popular systems include Fibonacci numbers, stochastics, volatility inversion, and divergence formulas. Many of these new systems feature special manipulation of price data. However, with the growth in programs that's occurring, you will likely soon see formulas that use a combination of price data and volume and open interest data.

10
Seasonals, Cycles and Your Trading Profits

Most commodities have a repetitive annual price pattern which is called the seasonal price cycle. Seasonal price trends are a reflection of regular annual changes in supply and demand factors. Seasonal price analysis is recognized by one of the stories in commodity trading folklore — the so-called voice from the tomb.

The story is about a very wealthy man who made a fortune skillfully trading commodities. He promised to reveal to his son the secret of his trading success after he died. When the probate judge opened the trader's strongbox, he found this message for his son: "Buy wheat near the seasonal lows during the summer. Sell wheat near the seasonal highs in the winter. Buy corn and soybeans near the seasonal fall lows and sell at the seasonal spring or summer highs."

While the voice-from-the-tomb story may be only legend, the principle is sound. Seasonal price patterns are regular repeated cycles which are a major market influence in nearly all commodities. The growing season causes seasonal patterns in crops; breeding and feeding patterns influence livestock seasonals; and the consumption habits of consumers can cause seasonal price patterns in the metals.

The seasonal crop pattern is probably the easiest to understand because of its association with the growing year. Price patterns of crops are influenced by anticipation before planting, weather problems during the growing season and the usual abundance at harvest. The odds are about 7 out of 10 that the lowest cash soybean, wheat and corn prices will come at harvest. The stored crop gains in value as consumption begins to reduce the available supply.

Seasonal patterns for livestock tend to be more complex than other commodities because of the joint dependency on feed grain prices as well as livestock production and consumption. As with crops, seasonal trends for livestock are primarily supply-oriented. Prices generally are depressed in the fall and spring when the supply of meat is the greatest. Cash prices usually rise into the winter and summer months when marketings taper off but demand is high. A more detailed analysis of seasonal price patterns for major agricultural commodities appears later in this chapter.

The repetitive price patterns for metals are caused by demand because these products aren't dependent on weather for development. Silver prices vary seasonally, primarily because of its photographic application. Gold prices usually soften in late summer when industrial users cut back on their manufacturing of jewelry. Almost half of all copper is used in electrical and heat conductivity. Unlike crops and livestock, the production rates of all metals are relatively constant. Their primary supply problems are related to unusual labor or political changes in producing countries.

Validate Seasonal Price Studies

The charts on the following pages are typical seasonal cash price tendencies for 20 commodities, based on research conducted by Clayton Commodities of St. Louis, Inc. Because your money is at stake, it's a good idea to update seasonal patterns to confirm the findings of previous studies or invalidate some patterns which many traders believe to be the expected seasonal pattern. Each trader should do his own research because there's much to be said for being in close touch with your work.

Systematically determining seasonal price patterns is time-consuming. The first step is finding the data for the markets you're interested in studying. A good source for studying average monthly cash prices for agricultural commodities is U.S. Department of Agriculture statistics. However, because your money is invested in the futures market and cash and futures prices can move in different directions, a study of seasonal trends in the futures market will be more indicative of what patterns to expect. Sources of futures price data are the yearbooks published by commodity exchanges.

The next step is studying seasonal charts showing the month-to-month differences for the number of years you have data. But, rather than stopping here as most seasonal studies do, go one step farther and analyze the reliability factor. This is an important item because it tells you the percentage of times the market follows the expected seasonal pattern.

The accompanying reliability chart of cash pork bellies is from MBH Commodity Advisors in Winnetka, Illinois. It shows that the September to October price slide pattern occurs 93% of the time. In other words, cash pork belly prices fall during September more than 9 years out of 10.

Other patterns, once believed to be reliable, are no better than the random walk. The July-August uptrend in bellies happens only 59% of the time, the MBH chart shows. This is not much better than the flip of the coin. Knowing these reliabilities improves your ability to make sound trading decisions.

From reliability studies of the cash markets, Jake Bernstein, president of MBH, found that the meats are generally the most reliable in following their seasonal patterns. The grains were a close second, but the metals were least reliable in following seasonal patterns consistently.

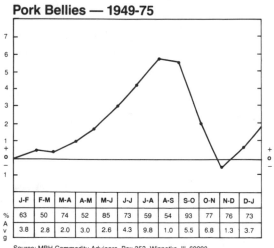

Pork Bellies — 1949-75

	J-F	F-M	M-A	A-M	M-J	J-J	J-A	A-S	S-O	O-N	N-D	D-J
%	63	50	74	52	85	73	59	54	93	77	76	73
Avg	3.8	2.8	2.0	3.0	2.6	4.3	9.8	1.0	5.5	6.8	1.3	3.7

Source: MBH Commodity Advisors, Box 353, Winnetka, Ill. 60093

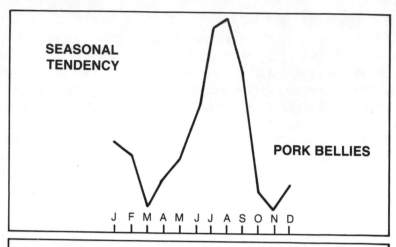

SEASONAL
TENDENCY

PORK BELLIES

J F M A M J J A S O N D

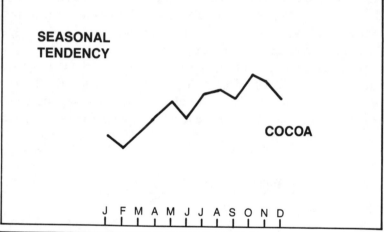

SEASONAL
TENDENCY

COCOA

J F M A M J J A S O N D

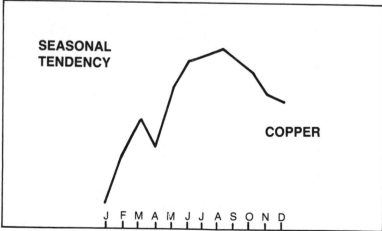

SEASONAL
TENDENCY

COPPER

J F M A M J J A S O N D

Source: Clayton Commodities of St. Louis, Inc.

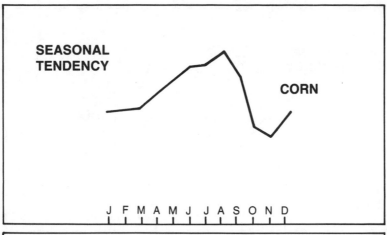

SEASONAL TENDENCY

CORN

J F M A M J J A S O N D

SEASONAL TENDENCY

SHELL EGGS

J F M A M J J A S O N D

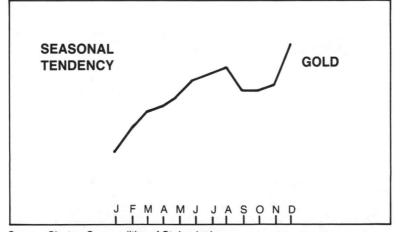

SEASONAL TENDENCY

GOLD

J F M A M J J A S O N D

Source: Clayton Commodities of St. Louis, Inc.

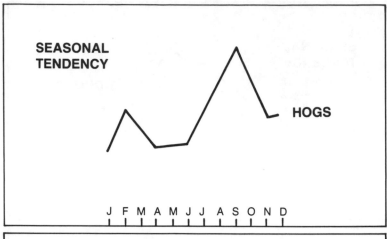

SEASONAL TENDENCY

HOGS

J F M A M J J A S O N D

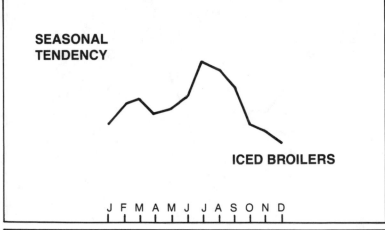

SEASONAL TENDENCY

ICED BROILERS

J F M A M J J A S O N D

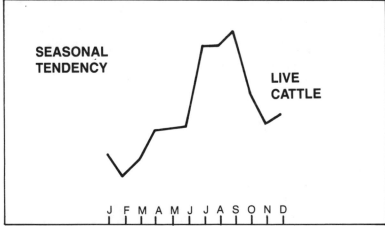

SEASONAL TENDENCY

LIVE CATTLE

J F M A M J J A S O N D

Source: Clayton Commodities of St. Louis, Inc.

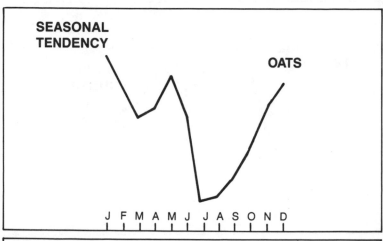

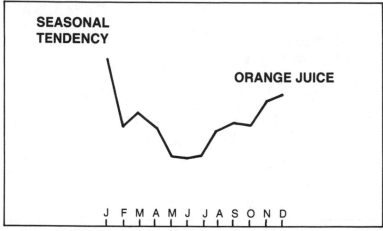

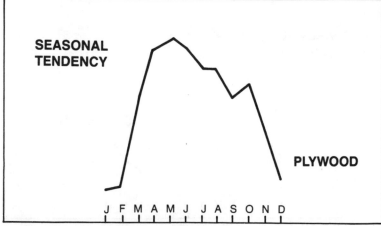

Source: Clayton Commodities of St. Louis, Inc.

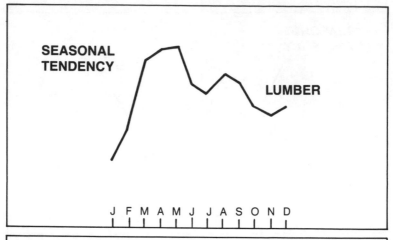

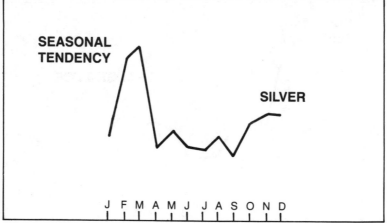

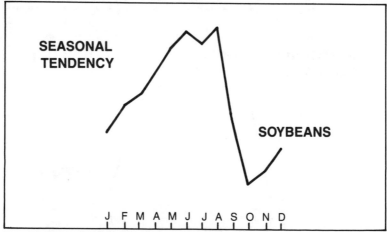

Source: Clayton Commodities of St. Louis, Inc..

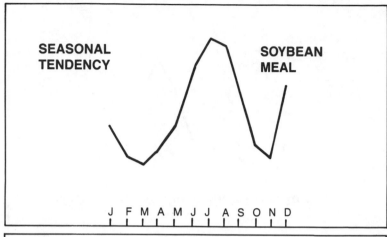

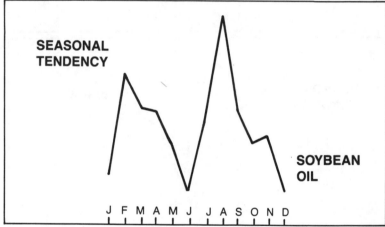

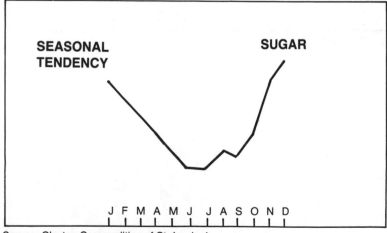

Source: Clayton Commodities of St. Louis, Inc.

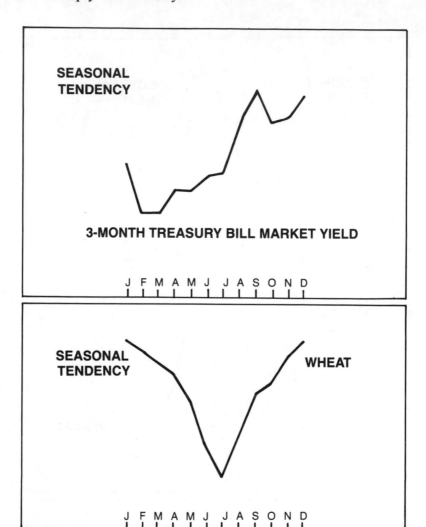

Source: Clayton Commodities of St. Louis, Inc.

Rarely Go Against the Seasonals

When a seasonal tendency has been isolated, you usually can determine the reason for its existence. As long as the reason exists in succeeding years, prices probably will repeat their performance. Based on historical data, the chances of being right are in your favor. This can greatly simplify your job of forecasting price trends if you think in terms of a normal seasonal pattern and then make whatever adjustments are necessary from the normal tendency.

The use of repetitive annual patterns in commodity trading can be profitable as long as you understand the limits as well as the strengths of this trading tool. Seasonals should not be relied on alone as the basis for making sales or purchases because they are not specific timing indicators. Seasonals will not tell you when to get into and out of a particular market.

But they serve as a guide when considering other factors. As a *general* timing tool, seasonals are valuable if combined with other technical and fundamental analysis. For example, if you know a seasonal downtrend is about to unfold in the midst of a bear market, you can be more confident about following the sell signals from other indicators.

Experienced traders do not go against reliable seasonal expectations without having a very good reason for doing so. A wise commodity trader follows one basic rule: Rarely buy a commodity after it has passed its seasonal highs; rarely sell a commodity after it has passed its seasonal lows.

Of course, seasonal price tendencies are not perfect. They do not happen the same every year. Keep in mind that seasonals represent history and do not necessarily predict the future.

Some researchers of seasonal trends place as much importance on contraseasonal trends as they do on the normal price pattern. When a well-established seasonal trend fails to materialize, it indicates a dramatic change in the traditional fundamental picture.

For example, cash corn prices normally trend lower during the harvest period. If this doesn't happen, it's a sure sign that either demand factors are stronger than usual or that the supply is smaller than earlier anticipated, or both. An unexpectedly small corn crop in 1983 caused prices to peak at harvest time. When this happens, you can throw the seasonals out the window. Short crops have long tails. A high price at harvest time will ration the limited supplies until the next crop is harvested.

Any seasonal tendency that becomes well-known is almost certain to be smoothed out as more and more traders act on it. Seasonal factors are constantly discounted at the Chicago Mercantile Exchange when spring and fall hog contracts trade at prices below the winter and summer months. The Chicago Board of Trade also moderates the violent seasonal price tendencies in grains.

Although futures trading has discounted highly reliable cash price tendencies, they are not completely eliminated. The futures market anticipates the cash market because of expected weather, expected production and expected demand. As painfully discovered by many traders, there is often a difference between the seasonals in the cash and futures markets. The few seasonal studies of the futures market show some marked differences from published seasonal patterns in the cash market.

The following seasonal studies of the major agricultural futures markets were researched by Walt Bressert, president of HAL Commodity Cycles, who studies the highs and lows of each month for the nearby futures contract until the last day of the month preceding delivery. Cash price studies normally are conducted using the monthly average price.

Cattle

The seasonal pattern in cattle depends on longer-term cycles. When the longer-term cycles are moving down, cattle prices will tend to top by July, and the seasonal lows are generally made during the fall months. Following the seasonal low, prices should not exceed season highs made earlier in the year.

But once longer-term cycles have bottomed and are moving up, the seasonal lows are made earlier. Instead of fall lows, the seasonal lows are made between June and September, when the cash market generally is making its seasonal crest. Futures prices normally will exceed the highs made earlier in the year as they move toward the crest of the next seasonal cycle in the longer-term cycle. In both cases, more than three-fourths of the seasonal highs are made between March and July. Seventy-five percent of the seasonal lows in futures are made during June through September.

The cattle futures market has been trading only since 1965 so the number of samples in this study is very limited. The seasonal studies for livestock futures should not be considered as reliable as the studies of grain futures. Normally, it is advisable to have at least 20 years or more of price data.

Corn

The difference between cash and futures seasonals is not as great in corn as it is in livestock. The typical seasonal pattern for cash prices shows an August peak followed by a low during the fall months.

The futures market doesn't follow exactly the same pattern. Futures tend to peak in midsummer ahead of cash prices and bottom about the same time as the cash market about half the time. In the other years, corn futures bottomed by August. Seasonal lows in August tend to be the rule in years when carryover surpasses a billion bushels. In years when production and carryover are overwhelmingly bearish, the futures market usually discounts this factor by August.

Hogs

Seasonal trends in the cash hog market probably are the most reliable of agricultural commodities. Cash prices repeatedly make their highs during the winter and summer months when demand is greatest and production is lowest. Prices decline into the spring and fall months when hog marketings increase. Nine years out of ten, cash prices trend lower during September.

But because the futures market anticipates cash trends, Bressert's study shows that two-thirds of the seasonal hog futures highs are made in May and June, which is ahead of the summer peak in the cash market. Bressert's study of the hog futures market shows that hog futures make their "fall" lows in August about 50% of the time. August is the critical month for the hog market. Following this month, one of three patterns normally occurs, depending on where prices are in longer-term cycles. Regardless of which pattern is followed, hog futures bottom between August and October 83% of the time.

Soybeans

The seasonal highs in the cash market usually come in August, and the seasonal lows are made during the harvest period. But the futures market has considerable lead time on the cash market.

The futures market follows one of two patterns. In one pattern, a peak in May is followed by the seasonal low by the end of August 70% of the time. The second pattern peaks in June-July with a 65% chance of a bottom in the September-November period.

Whichever pattern prices follow, more than two-thirds of the seasonal highs are made during April through July, and nearly 80% of the lows occur in August through November.

Wheat

The seasonal top in the wheat market occurs during November through January 73% of the time. If prices have been rising from a seasonal low and one of these months' lows drops below the preceding month's lows, there is a very high probability that the seasonal cycle has topped.

Prices in the futures market bottom during May through September 88% of the time. During this period, if a month's high exceeds the previous month's high, the seasonal low is confirmed with a very high probability.

Causes of Longer-term Cycles Aren't Known

The seasonal is a special case of a repetitive cycle every 12 months. Seasonal patterns are easier to find than other cyclical patterns since we know they repeat themselves each year.

Each commodity has its own longer-term cycles. The shortest useful cycle for the beginning trader is the seasonal cycle, which already has been covered. Other cycles may be 3, 5, or even 50 years from one low to the next. Probably the best known are the 11-year cattle cycle and the 3- to 4-year hog cycle. But the grains and metals also have longer-term cycles. Corn, for instance, has a very reliable 3½-year cycle that has repeated itself 32 times since 1860. This cycle was discovered by the Foundation for the Study of Cycles, a non-profit research organization which looks for recurring movement in everything from lynx population to stock prices.

While the causes of seasonal cycles are known, the causes of longer-term cycles are not always known. The theory of cyclical analyis is that events will occur within a cycle to move prices in the expected direction of the cycle.

A good example is silver. In 1971, silver was $1.30 per ounce. No fundamental information was available at that time to indicate the series of events that would push prices nearly 400% higher. But the cycles said prices were going higher because silver was at the bottom of a major 5½-year cycle. During the next three years, the Arab-Israeli war, oil embargo, devaluation, monetary fear, record inflation and high interest rates all pushed silver prices in the direction predicted by the cycle. The cycles called for higher prices, and the fundamentals unfolded to send prices to $6.40.

A basic problem with fundamental analysis is that the events causing changes in supply and demand often are not known until after the fact — well after tops and bottoms have occurred. All known fundamental information relative to supply and demand is in the market on the close of each day. The market usually moves before the fundamental reason for the move is fully known. Cycles can help you pick the direction of cash prices before the news comes out.

Detrending Methods Can Isolate Cycles

To isolate a cycle, you should have at least seven repetitions. Normally, you would like to have 20 or more. But for a cycle about 11 years long, such as the cattle cycle, 20 repetitions takes you back quite a ways so most cycle analysts settle for seven. For smaller cycles of less than one year, you should observe 40 repetitions.

Often, the reason cycles are not seen is because the interaction of many large and small cycles makes individual cycles hard to pick out. However, through the process of detrending, the effects of all cycles larger than the one to be studied can be eliminated.

To detrend price data, Bressert uses a moving average the same length as the suspected cycle and plots it on a chart with the price data. Instead of plotting the moving average at the current date, it is centered or plotted in the middle of the time period used to compute the moving average. In Figure 1, on the following page, the last 20 days of prices have been used to compute the moving average, and the moving average computed on Day 20 is plotted on Day 10. The moving average computed on Day 15 (using the previous 20 days) would have been plotted on Day 5.

Once the moving average has been computed and centered, the simplest method of detrending is to plot the actual distance of prices from the moving average. This has the advantage of requiring no additional mathematical calculations, once the moving average is computed.

As shown in Figure 2, the distance of prices from the moving average line can be measured with a ruler and plotted around a

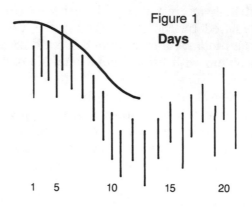

Figure 1
Days

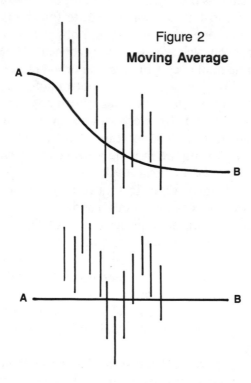

Figure 2
Moving Average

zero line directly below the prices for easy comparison. The distance of prices from the center of the moving average AB is measured and plotted around the straight line AB. Because price activity revolves around the moving average, a cycle the same length as the moving average can be seen without the effects of the longer cycles.

Look for Dominant Cycles on Weekly Charts

Knowing that cycles do affect futures prices is interesting information but not of much use in the markets unless a commodity can be analyzed to give a relatively accurate indication of future price activity.

To analyze a particular market, it is necessary to isolate the dominant cycles affecting price activity. A dominant cycle is one that visibly and consistently affects price activity. A nondominant cycle is one that seems to move in and out of price activity and is not always visible and is not consistent.

It is the dominant cycle that is used to analyze a market and to establish time and price expectations for the future. A very dominant cycle in agricultural commodities is the seasonal cycle. There are other cycles which are more dominant than the seasonal and often will determine the direction of a market for months or even years. Knowledge of these cycles is of great importance in both hedging and speculation.

Some of the dominant long-term cycles include the 67-month and 41-month corn cycles, the 39-month and 24-month soybean cycles, 9¼-year wheat cycle, 9¼- and 5½-year silver cycles, 5-year sugar cycle, 5¾-year cotton cycle, and the 6-year and 3-year meat cycles.

By knowing which cycles are affecting the markets, expectations can be established for future troughs and crests. As a general rule of thumb, you should allow a variation of plus or minus 10% of the length of the cycle when establishing expectations for futures tops and bottoms.

Cycles have become a popular trending aid in the last few years as a few advisory services base their trading recommendations almost entirely on their analysis of cycles.

While the most probable time for cycles to top and bottom can be established, cycles do sometimes stretch, shrink and, on occasion, disappear. Just because a cyclical pattern has worked well in the past is no guarnatee it will work well in the future.

We have scratched only the surface of cyclical analysis. There are many other cyclical factors, such as the activity of smaller daily cycles, which are beyond the scope of this book. For example, more than 30 identifiable corn cycles have been discovered by the Foundation for the Study of Cycles. Rather than become bogged down by all these smaller cycles, the average trader should be aware of longer-term cycles and seasonals as a general indicator for picking long-term trends.

11
Spread Trading

A futures trader who doesn't understand spreads is no better equipped to play the spread game than a baseball catcher who'd stand in front of Nolan Ryan without a face mask and chest protector.

Spreads are price differences between different contracts of one commodity such as December corn and July corn or between the same contracts of related commodities, such as February hogs and February pork bellies. If you hold a spread position, you are long one contract and short another. The risk to a spread trader is that, because of the different (lower) margin requirements, he will overtrade.

Spreaders enter positions when relationships are "out of line." They make money by liquidating positions when these relationships return to "normal". There are at least seven reasons spread trading may beat holding net positions.

1. *You can establish lower risk trades*. Storable commodities have carrying charges, which allow for the cost of interest, insurance and storage. When spread relationships include ample compensation for these charges, your trading risk essentially has been reduced to commission costs.

Having essentially reduced your trading risk to commission costs, you are able to hold on indefinitely. The longer you hold, the better your chances of profit.

2. *Gain leverage*. In the wild 1973 soybean market when futures eventually rose to more than $12 per bu., intracrop spread margins were only about one-fifth the amount of margin required for

outright positions. During that wild market, the September contract rose $6.60 per bushel. But the spread between September and November contracts widened $2.70 per bushel. If you traded five spreads instead of one net position, your gain would have been over twice as much as the net position holder, but margin requirements would have been the same.

3. *Reliable seasonal behavior.* Although net prices tend to follow well-documented seasonal patterns, some spread relationships follow seasonal patterns with even less fluctuation and greater reliability.

For instance, here are some pronounced seasonal tendencies in grain market spreads:

● August soybeans tend to gain on the new-crop November contract from October through May. August beans tend to lose on November from May through August.

● May corn tends to lose on July corn from harvest through the winter months. Then May corn tends to gain on July starting in early spring when the Great Lakes open. The tendency is for May to go to a premium over July at or before the delivery period.

● May wheat tends to gain on July wheat from summer through late winter and starts losing in March.

● July and September corn contracts tend to gain on the distant new-crop December contract soon after the December contract comes on the Board.

4. *Get on board established moves.* Occasionally, forward spreads begin to work only after a bull market move is well underway. For instance, in the major bull moves in cotton in 1973 and 1975-76, forward spreads began to work only after the market had made a substantial advance. The spreads still were available at a very reasonable risk:reward ratio, while net positions couldn't be taken without using very wide stops and high risk.

5. *Take advantage of changing relationships.* One example is spreads between two different crops. These spreads tend to work because of different production cycles for different crops. Wheat and oats, for instance, are harvested in the summer. Corn is harvested in the fall. Both wheat and oats tend to gain on corn from July to October and tend to lose value to corn from December to July.

6. *Spreading may suit your temperament better.* Traders who choose low-risk carrying charge spreads are immune to the day-to-day pressures of net trading. The more volatile the market, the

greater this advantage. Instead of the risk of price movement, the spreader has only the risk of spread relationship changes.

7. *Less risk of limit moves.* During times of limit moves, both sides of a spread will usually move the limit in one direction. This means no change in the profit position to the spread trader while half the holders of net positions are suffering tremendous losses.

Types of Spreads

Before taking this discussion of spreads farther, you have to become familiar with the terms. First, the four types of spreads:

● Interdelivery spreads. The long and short positions are in different contracts of the same commodity on the same exchange. Examples: May-July corn, September-November soybeans, March-May cotton. These are also called intramarket or intrafutures spreads. Note that in spread lingo, the long side of the spread always is listed first.

● Intermarket spreads. The long and short positions are taken in the same futures by different exchanges. Examples: Minneapolis vs. Chicago wheat, Kansas City vs. Chicago wheat, New York vs. London sugar.

● Interfuture spreads. Positions are taken in related futures such as pork bellies vs. hogs, wheat vs. corn, meal vs. oil. Futures do not have to be traded on the same exchange.

● Source-product spread. A position is initiated by taking one side in the commodity and offsetting positions in one or more of its products. The best example is the soybean crush spread — soybeans vs. meal and oil.

Besides the various types of spreads, spread traders use other specialized terms in their market lingo. Here are some of the terms:

Arbitrage: Usually a reference to intermarket spreading between two exchanges. An example: Chicago vs. Kansas City wheat.

Back spread: Long a distant month and short a nearby month.

Backwardation: An inverted market, with nearby contracts selling at a premium to distants.

Bear spread: Same as a back spread.

Butterfly spread: A three-legged spread in which the short (long) month is couched between two long (short) months.

Bull spread: Long in a nearby month and short in a distant month.

Carrying charges: The cost of storing a commodity over a period of time. Made up of three elements: physical storage costs, interest, and insurance on the commodity value. Interest is by far the most important component. A "carrying charge market" is one in which distant contracts are quoted at a premium to nearbys. This concept is applicable only to storable, nonperishable commodities.

Contango: A term referring to a carrying charge market.

Crush spread: Long soybeans vs. short oil and meal.

Inverted market: Nearby contracts are selling at a premium to distants.

Forward spread: Same as a bull spread.

Leg: One side of a spread.

Lifting a leg: Liquidating one side of a spread, leaving an exposed, outright (net) position open. This can be risky.

Limited risk spread: A forward spread trade taken near full carrying charges. In storable (nonperishable) commodities, the distant contract may bear a maximum premium over the nearby by no more than an amount sufficient to cover the full carrying charges.

Narrowing: A spread narrows when the nearby contracts are gaining on the more distant and narrowing from full carrying charges.

Normal market: Nearby contracts are at a discount to distants; the premium on distant contracts reflects partial or full charges.

Reverse crush spread: Long oil and meal vs. short soybeans.

Straddle: A term synonymous with the term spread.

Switch: A term synonymous with the term spread.

Widening: A spread is referred to as widening when the distant months are gaining on the nearbys. Example: Widening toward full carrying charges.

Unwinding: Liquidating a spread.

Even if you're firmly convinced you'll never trade spreads, a knowledge of how spreads work will make money for you on your net positions. Changes in spread relationships may signal the beginning or ending of major bull or bear price moves.

Spreads May Show You Market Bottoms

There is a very high correlation between side carrying charge markets and seasonal bottoms. Often spreads will be at their widest point just as the market makes its seasonal low. This is often caused by a washout in the nearby contract, which may take that contract to new lows while other contracts do not make new lows. As an example, deferred soybean oil contracts went to record premiums over nearbys in the mid-1970s. After that, both bull spreads and net long positions made sizeable amounts of money.

Inverse markets may forecast bull moves in advance. As the harvest is brought in, a near month premium in the early crop year often signals further tightness will develop later in the year.

The rationale for wide carrying charges at market bottoms and seasonal lows is simple. Seasonal bottoms are usually made near harvest time when the supply of commodities is the greatest and demand is often at low ebb. Spread relationships are the best indicators of the demand for the commodity. When spreads are near full carry, that's signaling light demand. It's telling the commercials to store because the market is paying them a maximum return for storage.

When the spreads start to narrow, the market is signaling there are buyers for the cash commodity. When spreads for storable commodities narrow, commercials are getting a lower return on their storage. The market is signaling them, "We want the cash commodity now."

If you see a sizeable rally in the market that is not accompanied by bull spreading — or gaining of nearby contracts over deferreds — this kind of rally often is technical in nature and may be due for a sizeable setback.

The opposite situation also is true. Sometimes after the market has made a bottom and rallied initially, it will set back. If the setback is accompanied by bull spreading, you have a very reliable indicator of good demand for the cash commodity. That demand will pull the futures higher. Usually it is a time to establish net long positions with confidence.

Spreads May Also Signal Market Tops

Bear spreading, or the gaining of deferred contracts relative to the nearbys, may signal the top of a market. For instance, during the 1977 soybean bull market, old-crop contracts gained relative to new-crop contracts while prices were making a sizeable advance. Then the market settled down into a wide congestion phase above the $10 area. By studying the net charts, there was practically no clue on which way the breakout would come. However, all the while prices were in a trading range, old-crop prices were steadily losing their premium. It was a clear signal that price levels would go lower.

Corn spreads were another market tip-off in 1977. Most contracts went to full carry as the important 4-year support level of $2.50 was broken on weekly charts. The widening of the spreads and the breaking of that support level ushered in an immediate 70¢ bear move.

Cash/Futures Spreads Tip Off Market Direction

This spread is more commonly called basis — the difference between futures and cash. In commodities it is the cash market, not the futures, that determines overall price levels. Because of this relationship, cash prices often move first. When you see a suddenly developing premium of the cash market to the futures market, you are usually getting a valid tip-off that futures will move higher. The cash market is like a rubber band. It often pulls the futures along behind. A steadily rising cash market will pull up a reluctant futures market. On the flip side, a steadily falling cash market will nearly always pull the futures market lower.

Conversely, if futures prices are in a congestion phase, cash prices are headed down, and the market is headed for a time of normal seasonal weakness, you usually can take net short positions with greater confidence than normal.

General Rules for Trading Spreads

By now, you are well aware of the principle of making money with spreads. For storable, nonperishable commodities, the principle is that nearby months will gain on distant months when prices are advancing. Near months will lose on distant months when prices are falling. This concept applies to corn, wheat, oats, soybeans and soybean products, plywood, sugar, cocoa, pork bellies, orange juice, cotton and copper.

Metals markets, other than copper, are obvious exceptions to the general rule. Gold, silver, platinum and also potatoes perform exactly opposite to this general rule. When overall price levels for these commodities are advancing, deferred contracts will usually gain on nearby contracts. In other words, if the market is rising, the spreads which make money are generally long the deferred months and short the nearby months. In declining markets, the money-making spreads are long the nearby months and short the deferred months.

Metals spreads move opposite to the general spread rule because there are large world stockpiles of these metals and changes in the value of gold, silver and platinum are not due to near-term tightness or surplus. Rallies are caused by changes in the public's concept of value. When overall values rise, it costs more to store these commodities. Back contracts rise to reflect these storage costs.

Nonstorable commodities may or may not follow the general rule. Many of the strongest bull markets in cattle are launched from inverse markets because discounted back contracts discourage hedging. That tends to discourage commercial feedlots from placing cattle.

Also, many of the "wrecks" in the cattle market are caused by an upward stairstep in cattle futures. With nearby futures at low levels and deferred contracts at high levels, commercial feedlots often are able to buy feeder cattle at low enough prices to hedge in good profits in the higher-priced deferred contracts.

Hogs seldom follow the general rule because there is no flexibility in adjusting the production cycle. Once pigs are born, they're locked into a production chain unlike cattle. Therefore, each month's production is really a separate crop. In hog markets, the spread trader's concern is how the fundamentals will affect different month's hog marketings.

In young bull markets in hog futures, the back contracts often will be the first to rally, and they will lead the way for front futures contracts.

Spreads for Beginners

The best spreads for beginners — and some pros also stay with them exclusively — are the limited risk or carrying charge spreads. Full carry is generally the maximum premium a deferred contract of a storable commodity can command over a nearby. It's roughly equal to the cost of taking delivery, holding the commodity for the length of time between the two expiration dates, then redelivering the commodity.

Full carry in the cotton market, for instance, may be about 100 points per month, depending on the interest rate. Hence, a long December/short March cotton spread initiated at 300 points to the

March would have a risk equal to the commission — if the spread didn't move. Even spreads which are not put on at full carry are limited risk spreads in the sense that the risk can be calculated. Few spreads actually reach full carry. That's because there are large numbers of traders willing to do the spread in large amounts because they can calculate risk precisely and are willing to take that risk.

Carrying charges are not fixed. They can vary over time. The main reasons for changes are rises or declines in the value of the commodity and also changes in interest rates. Most brokerage firms have a table showing how to calculate full carrying charges. However, a reasonable rule of thumb is to double the prime interest rate. When the prime rate is 12%, for instance, the cost of storage for one year will be about 24%. That means if cotton is 80¢, then 24% or 19.2¢ will be one year's carrying charge. Broken down on a monthly basis, carrying charges will be 160 points per month. A maximum carrying charge for a limited risk trade might be about 75% of full carry, or about 120 points in this case.

Two Limited Risk Spreads

Two of the best examples of limited risk spreads that tend to work every year on a seasonal basis are the May/July corn spread and the May/December copper spread. The low for the May/December copper spread almost always is made in the year-end

May-December Copper Spreads					
Year	Low Date	Low Price	High Date	High Price	Gain from Date of Low
1965	12/30	150 May	4/22	1150 May	+ $2500
1966	12/25	280 May	4/12	1190 May	+ $2275
1967	11/17	210 May	1/1	320 May	+ $ 275
1968	11/15	480 May	3/23	1540 May	+ $2650
1969	10/30	110 May	4/26	900 May	+ $2000
1970	1/24	340 May	4/19	690 May	+ $ 875
1971	11/30	210 Dec	3/31	Even	+ $ 525
1972	12/9	140 Dec	12/22	80 Dec	− $ 150
	4/28	190 Dec			
1973	1/2	230 Dec	4/8	455 May	+ $1712
1974	1/15	360 May	1/30	1660 May	+ $3250
1975	11/8	490 Dec	2/20	350 Dec	+ $ 350
1976	11/2	360 Dec	4/8	230 Dec	+ $ 325
1977	4/7	300 Dec	1/5	270 Dec	− $ 225
1978	4/23	390 Dec	1/11	310 Dec	− $ 200
1979	11/30	380 Dec	2/7	70 May	+ $1125

period while the high for the year nearly always is made in the early spring.

Data compiled by former ContiCommodity Services spreads expert Phil Tiger shows that the spread often is near full carry during the initiation period, offering very low risk. Average profit from the low to high of the spread has been about $1,200 per contract. There are several years in which the spread showed a loss, but all losses were relatively small.

The May/July corn spread has been a very reliable performer if initiated in the historical support area of 4¢ premium to the July. The spread is usually placed during the post-harvest December-February period and is liquidated in April. In 1973, the May premium was over 14¢ per bu., resulting in an $800 profit per contract if the May/July spread was initiated in the post-harvest period when the July was at a 2¢ premium to the May.

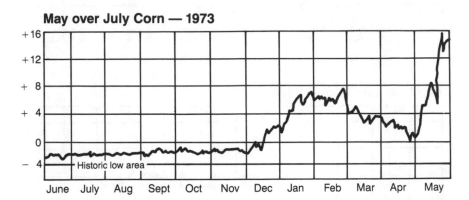

May over July Corn — 1973

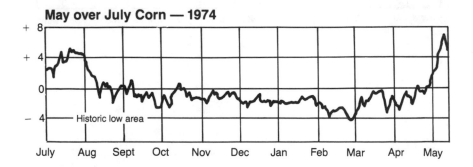

May over July Corn — 1974

May over July Corn — 1975

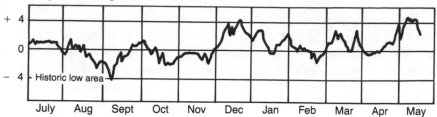

May over July Corn — 1977

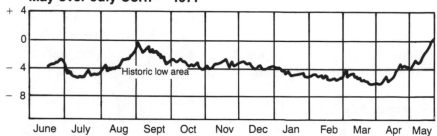

May over July Corn — 1978

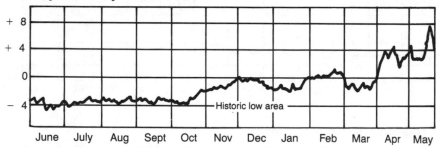

12
Interest Rate, Stock Index and Currency Futures

Agricultural futures are about grain, oilseeds, livestock, tropicals and cotton; financial futures are about money and the cost of money. Precious metal futures relate more to money than the cost of production or the demand by the industries that use gold, silver, platinum, and palladium.

Financial futures relate to money, but they do so in sightly different ways. Each segment is discussed in more detail in the chapters that follow.

There are interest rate futures (which are further divided into short-term and long-term instruments) concerned with the price (cost) of money.

These are those which relate to changing dollar values. The most obvious example is foreign currencies; gold and silver and, to a lesser extent, platinum also register changing values.

The last segment is the various index futures, but particularly the well-known stock indices. Other index futures are only recently introduced or are about to be introduced and relate to special segments of the economy like housing starts or utility stock prices.

It has to be recognized that the cost of money influences all transactions. Any trades for grains or cattle, cotton or sugar, equities or debt instruments are all concerned with the cost of money. It is pervasive. The international trade in commodities may be looked at as a way of moving money and not the other way around. In fact, money has been called the "ultimate commodity."

Options on the various features are another tool to manage the risks that are a part of every business. In popular terminology, an option provides the buyer with the right, but not the obligation, to buy or sell the underlying "commodity" be it sugar, soybeans, index or T-bond futures. For that right the buyer pays the seller a premium which may and does change in value.

All futures markets exit because there is uncertainty. If there was no risk of loss accompanying an opportunity to make a profit, there would be no need for futures markets. The risks associated with raw material markets have been well described before and need not be repeated here.

The risks associated with money have been around even longer; however, since 1934 and until 1971, the American dollar — the foremost currency in world trade — was tied to gold. They were interchangeable for citizens of other countries (American citizens could not own gold until 1974) at a fixed rate. The U.S. Treasury would pay $35.00 per ounce for gold and sell it at the same price. There were minor adjustments in that price from 1968 onward, but still the price between countries was only $42.00 per ounce when the gold/dollar bond was broken in August 1971.

It not only introduced variability in the value of the dollar, but it represented a weakening of the dollar. As inflation came to the forefront of the world's attention, it was obvious it would affect interest rates. Who would lend dollars today to be paid back tomorrow in dollars worth half as much? Many institutions had such contracts on their books and it is to the credit of the various exchanges that their members devised the futures markets and permitted financial institutions to continue to fund capital investments and foreign trade because they now had tools with which to manage their risks.

Interest Rate Futures . . .
Hot Market of the '80s

Interest rate futures have had a spectacular growth ever since their beginning in 1975. It was not only the increase in the volume of trade, but more importantly the number of debt instruments which could support active futures trading.

It is essential to understand that the underlying cash market (bonds, bills, GNMAs) is a direct obligation of the U.S. government GNMAs are an obligation of the Government National

At The Chicago Board Of Trade

	U.S. Treasury bonds	10 year Treasury notes	GNMA (CDR)*
Trading Unit	Face value $100,000 bonds not maturing or callable for 15 years	Face value $100,000 maturing 6½ - 10 years from delivery date based on 8%	$100,000 principal balance 8% GNMA certificate of 12-year duration
Price Quotation	Percentage of par e.g. 94-01 or 94 1⁄32 = $94,031.25	Percentage of par	Percentage of par
Minimum Fluctuation	1/32 of a point or $31.25 per contract	1/32 of a point	1/32 of a point
Daily Price Limit	64/32 or $2,000 above or below previous settlement	64/32 or $2,000 above or below previous settlement	64/32 or $2,000 above or below previous settlement
Hours of Trading (Chicago Time)	8:00 a.m. to 2:00 p.m.	8:00 a.m. to 2:00 p.m.	8:00 a.m. to 2:00 p.m. *Collateralized Depositary Receipt

At The International Monetary Market

	Three-month Eurodollar time deposit	Three-month domestic certificate of deposit	Three-month U.S. Treasury bill
Trading Unit	$1,000,000	$1,000,000	$1,000
Price Quotation	IMM Index difference between yield and 100; e.g. 8.50% yield = 91.50	IMM Index	IMM Index
Minimum Fluctuation	.01 (1 basis point) $25 per point	.01 (1 basis point) $25 per point	.01 (1 basis point) $25 per point
Daily Price Limit	1.00 (100 basis points) $2,500. No spot month limit	.80 (80 basis points) $2,000	.60 (60 basis points) $1,500
Hours of Trading (Chicago Time)	7:30 a.m. to 2:00 p.m.	7:30 a.m. to 2:00 p.m.	8:00 a.m. to 2:00 p.m.

Mortgage Association and carries with them the full faith and credit of the U.S. government).

In all cases, the futures are <u>not</u> an obligation of the U.S. government as a "party to every trade." The Clearing Corporation guarantees the opposite side of the transaction while the positions remain open.

The settlement for the Eurodollar future is cash. There is no underlying instrument to be delivered. The domestic certificates of deposit are "no name" CDs with detailed specifications as to maturity dates and accrued interest. U.S. Treasury bills with 91 days to maturity satisfy that contract.

Basics of Interest Rate Futures

The details of the major interest rate futures were set out so that you can become familiar with the terms. At the outset, there are three basics.

1. The rate of interest on a bond is not to be confused with its yield to maturity. There is an inverse relationship between interest rates and bond prices. An outstanding bond will decline in price whenever interest rates rise, and conversely.

2. Understand the meaning of the "yield curve." It is a graphic representation between yields of bonds with different maturity dates (but of approximately the same quality). Higher yields reflect higher risk. The longer the time period until maturity, the greater the risk to the bond holder.

There are times when the "yield curve" is flat (i.e. interest rates are about the same for differing maturities). It can be flat, but interest rate levels may still rise or fall.

With a change in yield (up or down), the longer maturity instruments will have a much greater change in price than their shorter term counterparts. To illustrate this, keep in mind that a basis point on $1,000,000 of *91-day* bills is $25. A basis point is 1/100 of 1 percent, or decimally, .0001. Thus, $1,000,000 × .0001 = $100 which is the amount a *1-year* bill would change with a change in price of 1 basis point. A 91-day bill would change by 100 ÷ 4 = $25, or one-fourth the change in 1-year bills. If a gain, the gain is one-fourth; and if a loss, the loss is one-fourth.

On examination of the above, it is easy to see why maturities are shortened in a falling market and lengthened in a rising one.

The job of the portfolio manager is to anticipate the next change in the yield curve and to decide which of the various maturities will provide maximum income or the smallest loss.

3. Recognize that interest rate futures are quoted in terms of an index. Note the first basic which was the inverse relationship of interest rates and market value. If futures quotations were the actual rate of interest, a lower interest rate would be higher than offers. To resolve this, the index is based on the difference between the actual yield and 100.00. A T-bill yielding, say, 10.5% would be quoted at 89.50. If a contract was bought at that price and subsequently went to 91.00, the buyer has a gain of 150 basis points.

The seller has a loss of the same amount. It results in the usual bid/offer relationship. If rates are expected to fall, futures will be bought since the dollar price will increase, and conversely.

The same thing is accomplished in the other interest rate futures that are quoted as a percentage of par. For example, Treasury bonds, notes, and GNMAs.

As indicated before, the users of money have both short- and long-term needs and goals. What can a corporate treasurer do to minimize his risk? When interest rate changes were relatively small in magnitude and few in number, the rate (for all practical purposes) was established. The lending banks undertook the risk and accepted the consequences if a higher rate of interest subsequently prevailed. Corporations and all major borrowers recognized the converse.

When interest rate changes increased dramatically in the 1970s, it was the advent of interest rate futures that permitted both the borrower and lender to protect their respective positions.

A corporate treasurer — or any prospective borrower — will determine if his needs are for the shorter term or the longer one. If the former, Treasury bills and commercial paper are traded; if the latter (and they are of intermediate length) Treasury notes are used. Long-term requirements are met in the GNMAs and Treasury bonds.

Corporations that borrow money run the gamut from airlines to zinc manufacturers. They are concerned with everything from agriculture to zoology, from the largest conglomerates to the smaller business. Borrowers include municipalities. The funds they use are provided by commercial banks, finance companies, savings and loan associations, trust and pension funds, insurance companies and investment bankers.

All of them can and will use the market for hedging and cross-hedging purposes, but only after determining their degree of exposure to a change of interest rates if the risk is hedgeable. What degree of exposure can be accepted is largely determined by corporate policy and personal outlook. It may be that the instrument used to represent and convey the funds does not have good correlation with the existing futures. And there may be other methods to gain some protection through the cash and forward markets.

As a trader, you will want to know about the underlying instrument, its origin and role in the money market, and what influences it. While there are different influences on short- and long-term markets, there are some fundamentals about which it is well to be informed.

The fundamental of all fundamentals applies to the cost of money and that is that interest rates are subject to the push/pull of supply and demand. If the cost of borrowing money exceeds the expected rate of return from the use of the funds, there is no incentive to borrow and the costs of borrowing will decline. The greater the expectations of return on those borrowed funds, the greater the demand for those funds and, therefore, the result will be higher rates. From the lenders' point of view there must be enough compensation; otherwise, there is no incentive to defer the use of the money from current consumption.

This is really not the place to go into an exhaustive study of the influence of the Federal Reserve Board which largely determines the availability of credit from commercial banks. There are long-term factors and influences of which you want to be aware. Every newspaper (financially or otherwise oriented) carried almost daily stories on the actual or projected size of U.S. government budget deficits. The same is true for the value of the dollar, economic growth rates, and inflation rates. As the price of money reflects the demand for money relative to the supply, these longer-term factors are important.

Traders, however, can lose their speculative funds in the short term while waiting for the "long term" to arrive. What influences interest rate futures are the reports of the money supply, federal funds and prime lending rates, and the major economic indicators like Wholesale and Consumer Price Indexes and the Index of Leading Economic Indicators.

The use of these futures is based on a relatively simple principle.

Anyone who has a position in the underlying instrument has undertaken a risk based on the potential for an interest rate change. Those who hedge are not limited to the instruments for which there are futures. High corporate bond rates can be offset with the opposite transaction in U.S. Treasury bonds and certainly mortgage rates will reflect their fluctuations in the GNMAs.

As indicated above, there are long-term instruments, short-term instruments and, therefore, corporate treasurers tend to look at short-term funding and long-term funding. In each case, the opportunities exist to offset the potential increase in funding cost and/or depreciation in the value of the assets held. The individual speculators are those who not only take a view of the market but are well aware of the yield curves and how they work.

There are shorter-term speculators who may spread between months in the same future or between the different interest rate futures. For example, there is quite a lot of activity between the bills and the bonds. The individual speculator can use the futures in lieu of the cash market. For example, even though a trader is aware of a potential rise in interest rates, it is difficult financially and mechanically for individuals to go short bonds. T-bond futures provide the opportunity to profit from either a rise or fall in interest rates. It should be noted that a wrong decision results in a loss.

Some speculatively minded traders put on a spread between nearby and deferred months in an interest rate future, or between different but related futures. As a example of the former, the spread between December 1984 T-bills (IMM) and September 1985 might well reflect short-term financing costs and may indicate the direction of private short-term interest rates. An example of the latter case would be T-bonds (CBT) versus GNMAs, both of which are concerned with longer maturity instruments.

Stock Index Futures . . . Newest Trader Tool

Stock index futures are also a tool of risk management. Traders of individual stocks are expected to know the facts about the company whose stock is being traded and the relationship of the national economy to that particular industry. Portfolio and fund managers with their various mixes of equities and debt instruments run into a higher order of risk.

It might be well to approach the use of stock index futures (and options on such futures) by pointing out the problems faced by holders of such equities before these new risk management tools were available. Not everyone is a manager of a portfolio of stocks with a combined value of $100,000,000 made up, say, from the shares of 20 major companies, but it is easier to describe the problems and their actual and potential solutions given those circumstances. If you own stock in one company, you certainly can consider trading in index futures; however, as a speculator you will want to know what the trade is doing. The "trade" is the portfolio manager.

Insofar as stock markets, like all other markets, have their major up and down moves, imagine the risk that a portfolio manager has when he/she thinks stock prices — the prices of the 20 stocks in the portfolio — will decline.

Once his/her mind was made up (in the pre-index days) that equity prices would go down, the only choice was to sell the stocks (or part of them) in the portfolio, which raised the cash position in the portfolio.

Physical stock options were available and the equity manager could either buy "puts" or write "calls" against the inventory. If a "put" was bought, then the manager had purchased the right to sell the stock at a certain price. If the price of the stock declined below that certain price, the option to sell would be exercised.

If the call was written, the manager was selling for cash the right of the buyer to buy stock at a certain price. If the price of the equity declined, the option would not be exercised and the fund manager had money to make up for the decline in stock prices while still holding onto the stock.

What may be hard to visualize now is the time it took to arrive at the justifiable decisions. One had to do intensive research into the individual company's financial makeup and the health of the industry of which it was a part to make the sell/not sell decision. It was at least as time consuming to decide whether the proper course was to buy a put or write a call and on which stocks in the portfolio. Each of those decisions could be translated into a costly transaction. Some stocks might be less liquid than others and selling large amounts would distort the price of the stock. In some cases, tax implications did not permit a sale, and in other cases, wholesale abandonment of such a portfolio was just not responsible nor was it possible.

Index Futures Allow Quick Action

The index futures permitted the portfolio manager to take rapid action. First of all, a sale of an index future in the appropriate amounts immediately reduced the exposure of the portfolio to market declines. Second, there was distortion in any of the underlying stock and, last, the cost of selling the index future and subsequently repurchasing it is lower than the cost of selling and repurchasing all or part of the underlying individual stocks. The portfolio continued to receive dividends.

As with all futures-related transactions, there are some potentially adverse effects which the portfolio manager recognizes. For example, one or more stocks in the portfolio may have changed its intrinsic value and selling the index future will not eliminate that risk. A futures market position is marked to the market at the close of business each day and that requirement is different from the money requirements generated by changing stock prices.

Most Active Stock Index Futures

	NYSE Composite	S&P 500*	Major Market Index futures	Value Line*
Where Traded	New York Futures Exchange (NYFE)	Index & Option Market Division of Chicago Mercantile Exchange	Chicago Board of Trade	Kansas City Board of Trade
Trading Unit	$500 times Index	$500 times Index	$100 times Index	$500 times Index
Minimum Fluctuation	.05 (5 basis pts.) or $25	.05 (5 basis pts.) or $25	1/8 pt. (1 pt. equals $100) or $12.50	.05 (5 basis pts.) or $25
Daily Price Limit	None	50 basis pts. or $2,500	None	None
Hours of Trading	10:00 a.m. to 4:15 p.m. New York time	9:00 a.m. to 3:15 p.m. Chicago time	8:45 a.m. to 3:15 p.m. Chicago time	9:00 a.m. to 3:15 p.m. Kansas City time

*Each index has a smaller version. The "mini" Value Line is $100 times that index; the S&P 100 is $200 times its index.

In 1984, the Chicago Board of Trade instituted trading in the Major Market Index which previously was calculated only in the American Stock Exchange (AMEX). The most well-known index is the Dow Jones Industrial Index. The proprietors have resisted every effort by the various exchanges to create a futures contract using that index. The Kansas City Board of Trade was the first to trade an index future. It is based on the Value Line Index.

Subsequently, the Chicago Mercantile Exchange inaugurated the Standard & Poors (S&P) 500 and later the S&P 100. In the former, the value is 500 times the index itself. If the index closed today at 180, then the value of one contract of the S&P 500 is $90,000. The S&P 100 is 200 times the index and would then have a value of $36,000. The activity in the S&P 100 has not kept pace with the S&P 500.

Name	Exchange	Index Value (Aug. 3, 1984)	Index Future Close (Aug. 3, 1984) -September-	Basis
S&P 500	CME	162.35	164.30	+1.93
S&P 100	CME	162.35	163.90	+1.53
NYSE Composite	NYFE	93.23	94.75	+1.52
Value Line	KCBOT	177.30	182.45	+5.15
Major Mkt. Index	CBOT	235.75	238.50	+2.75

The data used in the above table followed three hectic stock trading days, culminating in a record volume for the NYSE. The Dow Jones Industrial Average had increased 36 points in one day and over 75 points in three days.

For speculators then, the use of any of the major index futures is an excellent and convenient way to participate in the changes in equity markets.

A contract in the S&P 500 now requires minimum margin of about $6,000 with many FCMs requiring more. The 1-day change in the S&P 500 Index September future at the close of business August 3, 1984, was up 6.05 which means a gain to the longs of $3,025 per contract and oppositely to those who were short. To give that some perspective, a 5,000-bu. contract of soybeans has a 1-day limit of 30¢ per bu., or $1,500 per contract. The Value Line Index increased 7.75 for that day while the NYSE Composite Index increased 3.60. Both of those contracts are also valued at 500 times the index; however, a glance at each index value will disclose the dollar difference in each contract.

It is essential to study the stocks underlying each index to ferret out why the different indexes showed different responses to the surge in stock buying. If you try to equate the index futures to the DJIA, then you must also look at the makeup of that index. It has only 30 stocks in it; the S&P has 500 and the Composite all NYSE trading stocks. The MMI has 20 stocks.

Choosing the Right Index

The choice for the individual speculator might depend more on the size of the margin required for the contract. For example, an investor who would purchase $50,000 in stocks must commit $25,000 as initial margin. To control a dollar value almost as large in the Standard & Poors 500 with an index value as shown in the table would require only $6,000. For the New York Stock Exchange Composite Index, the initial margin of $3,500 for one contract would be sufficient. The new Major Market Index (CBOT) would require two contracts with minimum margin about $3,000. The total is $6,000.

The reasons for speculation is basically that one has a view of equity markets. There is liquidity in the index futures and the speculator can evaluate fundamental and technical data that enables him or her to make intelligent market decisions. It is important to recognize that each of the stock index futures contracts incorporates differences in its structure. In some ways the different market index futures permit spreading based on your knowledge of the makeup of the different indexes. For example, the Major Market Index trade in the Chicago Board of Trade is comprised of 20 "blue chip" stocks. The Kansas City Value Line Index follows about 1,700 stocks. Because some of the Value Line Index is unweighted and includes stocks of "second tier issues," they may well experience greater price variation than the more highly capitalized issue.

There is another side to that coin when the enthusiasm is not on the "buy" side. There are options on the stock index futures that can be used in conjunction with the futures. Those who are inclined to the "buy" side can minimize their risk by purchasing puts (the right to sell at a certain price). Each investor is obligated to work with his broker to find what is the index future that most suits his speculative methods and objectives.

The Rise of Currency Trading

In the mid-1980s, the United States dollar moved to new highs against every major currency. What this really proved was dollars, like every other commodity, is subject to the laws of supply and demand. United States currency is the premier trading currency and, for that reason, there is a huge supply overseas.

As always, prices relate supply relative to demand. In the mid-'80s, U.S. dollars were returning to the United States. They may be used by their owners for whichever investment or debt service they find most suitable. Interest rates in this country over that period of time attracted a substantial amount of dollars. U.S. government securities backed by the full faith and credit of the country provided a safe return of 12% to 14% over a period of months. An upsurge in equity markets is also a reflection of demand from abroad (along with, obviously, a pent-up demand from the managers of many large funds in this country). In any case, the dollars were attracted back to this country and the U.S. dollar was strong relative to other currencies.

In the fall of 1978, for example, the opposite was true. The U.S. dollar was being quoted at the lowest values (relative to all the major currencies) that had been seen either before or since.

If you were a seller of U.S. goods for which you were to receive British pounds now, you would have to decide how to calculate your actual cost and potential returns. For example, if you made the contract in January 1984 for shipment and payment in June 1984, you would have been exposed to profit erosion of 7% for each dollar.

Prior to the advent of foreign exchange futures, a seller would have protected himself in the forward market through a bank which extended a line of credit to him. The seller would have calculated the reception of British pounds at the time of sale and sold them to the bank six months forward at the rate provided by the bank. That cost was included in the original calculation.

With foreign exchange futures, the seller would have hedged his position by selling British pounds for the equivalent amount in the June or July contract. As pounds declined in value (relative to the dollar) the short sale will show a profit more or less offsetting the loss. It is no different than hedging an inventory of grain. If you plan to receive currency other than dollars (that increases your inventory), then sell the future. As the actual currency is received, you sell it to the bank for dollars. You are reducing your inventory. As you reduce inventory, cover (buy in) in equivalent amounts the futures previously sold.

What Factors Influence Currencies

The factors that influence foreign currencies may be categorized as follows:

1. Governmental influence
2. Balance of payments
3. Seasonal fluctuations
4. Individual expectations.

You might note that, of the four categories, only one tends to be subject to measurement. Every country has a balance of payments which may be in default or in surplus. In the briefest description, if the country's balance of payment surplus is increasing, the demand for that country's currency is also increasing. If a deficit exists and it is growing, then the currency is less desirable in world markets. It takes time to sum up the balance of payments. At the end of a fiscal year, there are the transactions which include the export of goods and services, foreign investments, imports of goods and services, and transactions of the country's central banks which all add up to the country's balance of payments. What has to be understood is that all those imports and exports of goods and services relate to incomes of the private sector. It is the money that is available to be spent. Obviously, countries with lower levels of income cannot purchase as much nor invest as much in other countries.

Another factor is the general level of prices. If U.S. automobile prices or steel prices reach a level at which other countries can ship us automobiles or steel, they will. The third influence is interest rates. The strength in the United States dollar is a direct result of the high rates of interest available to purchasers of U.S. government securities. Their money flows to the United States. This is a form of investment on the part of the buyer.

Government Actions No. 1 Trade Factor

The most important factor is governmental influence. It is not possible to overemphasize its importance. There are the activities which are internal and generally summed up as domestic monetary policies and the control of the availability of money. Internal policies have to do with being elected and reelected. External policies have to do with the International Monetary Fund and Exchange controls. To sum up, government action is not susceptible to ordinary analysis.

There are trade treaties, subsidies, import taxes, domestic tax policy. Investors from overseas look at a country's political stability and, where they are not satisfied, they will not invest. It is easier to see political instability in the developing countries but, on the other hand, there are degrees of instability in even the most advanced industrial nations of the world. There are economic policy changes that go along with the change in political parties.

Seasonal fluctuations were mentioned and this can be related to the cycle of importing and exporting agricultural goods or other goods that relate to climate; for example, crude petroleum.

As far as expectations go, all of the other factors are involved, but investors have to make their own decisions which lead to the generalized expectation. It is possible for the world's investors to anticipate a change in the Fed funds rate that would suggest a tightening or easing of interest rates. Currencies would begin to flow relative to the dollar based on those expectations.

It is not difficult to point out that those who are buying or selling goods in forward position need to protect themselves against a major change in foreign exchange rates. There are, however, other kinds of situtations where understanding relative values is important. There are companies who build plants abroad and companies which finance overseas companies. They may be purchasers or sellers of equities in foreign countries. It is the necessity of planning financial operations in and with other currencies that requires knowledge of the trend of the relationship of other major trading currencies to the U.S. dollar.

Speculators in foreign currencies can, of course, do technical analysis which should be encouraged. As indicated, there are fundamentals which, when taken into account with the technical analysis, will provide the best outcome. Those who are looking for fundamental information that affects all the currencies must be aware that the volume of statistical information is fantastic for each of the countries whose currencies are traded at the IMM. There is almost the same amount of information that comes from the United States government. The exceptions are Mexico where the information available is restricted and the Netherlands where the reports lag the event by many more months than is prevalent elsewhere. In brief, there are the reports of every economic indicator including the aforementioned balance of payments. Only a partial listing includes retail and wholesale sales, consumer and wholesale price indexes, and factory and durable goods orders just to name a few. Nothing, however, is more important than the activities of government itself.

The contracts in foreign currency now being traded at the IMM are always quoted in terms of the U.S. dollar which means that the price applies to a unit of foreign currency. The quotation is in "points."

The number of foreign currency units (e.g., pounds or Swiss francs) per contract is given in the left hand corner. The decimal equivalent of the minimum fluctuation is the second column. When the first is mutiplied by the second, the result is the U.S. dollar value which is the third column. The fourth column is the dollar value of a 1-point move and the last column then is the minimum fluctuation in points (Column 3 divided by Column 4).

Key Statistics For Currencies

	Units per Contract	Decimal Equivalent of Minimum Fluctuation	Dollar Value	Dollar Value of One Point	Minimum Moves in Points
British Pound (BP)	25,000	$.0005	$12.50	$ 2.50	5
Deutsche Mark (DM)	125,000	.0001	12.50	12.50	1
Swiss Franc (SF)	125,000	.0001	12.50	12.50	1
Canadian Dollar (CD)	100,000	.0001	10.00	10.00	1
Japanese Yen (JY)	12,500,000	.000001	12.50	12.50	1
Dutch Guilder (DG)	125,000	.0001	12.50	12.50	1
French Franc (FR)	250,000	.00005	12.50	2.50	5

13
Options

Through the years another risk management tool has been developed. Options were first traded on the physical goods. Without
going into a lengthy history, there were and are two kinds of
options. A *call* option gives the buyer of that option the right, but
not the obligation, to buy the physical goods at a specified price at
any time during the life of that option. Obviously the buyer of the
"call" protects himself against an upward movement in prices.

A *put* option gives the buyer the right, but not the obligation, to
sell the physical goods at the specific price at any time during the
life of the option. A buyer of a "put" is protecting his inventory
against declining prices.

The buyer of the put or call pays the seller a premium for
undertaking that risk. If the buyer of the call finds that the goods on
which he bought the call did not go up, then his cost is the premium.
If the buyer of the put finds that the price did not decline, then his
cost is the premium.

The seller is known as the writer of the option, and obviously is
willing to undertake the risk that prices (in the case of a call) will
not go up, and in the case of a put will not go down. Frequently, the
option writer writes both puts and calls.

The price at which the put or call will be exercised is called the ·
strike price. It is the price at which the buyer of the call has the right
to purchase the goods. It is also the price at which the buyer of a put
has the right to sell the goods. It is also referred to as the exercise
price.

In very recent times it has become permissible to have options on futures contracts rather than the physical commodity which underlies the futures. The buyer of a call has the right to buy a future (to go long) and the buyer of a put has the right to sell (that is, to go short) at specified futures prices during the life of the option.

The Fundamentals Of Options

	Call	Put
Buyer	Right to buy futures	Right to sell futures
Writer or Seller (if exercised)	Must sell futures	Must buy futures

What has to be understood and kept firmly in mind is that trading in call options is completely separate and distinct from trading in put options. The reason that is important is that a buyer of an option on a futures contract can liquidate his option by selling an identical option at anytime prior to expiration. The important word is *identical*. One may buy a call and sell a call, which will liquidate his position in calls if the expiration date and strike price are the same. If he were to buy a call and buy a put, he would have two separate positions which would not be self-liquidating.

Options and where they are traded at this time, along with their volume, is shown below.

Options now traded	Jan.-Aug. 1984 Volume of trade (Contracts)
Chicago Board of Trade Bonds	4,261,571
COMEX Gold	914,463
CS & CE Sugar	6,491
Index and Options Market S&P 500	433,046
NYFE Stock Exchange Index	174,659
Deutsche Mark	404,532
MidAmerican Gold	19

It is apparent that the interest in Treasury bonds options far exceeds any other option. Only the sugar option and the Mid-America gold are at levels that raise questions about their viability.

The Commodity Futures Trading Commission in 1984 authorized the trading of options on certain agricultural commodities. The Chicago Board of Trade now trades options on soybean and wheat futures and the Kansas City Board of Trade has options of wheat futures. The Cotton and Orange Juice Exchange has options on cotton and the Chicago Mercantile Exchange has options on cattle and hogs. It would seem likely that options on corn futures will not be far behind. Some of the possibilities are discussed even though some rule changes could (and probably will) occur.

In discussing options of futures, the only thing negotiated between the buyer and seller is the premium. What influences the value of that premium is what the whole subject of options is about. It is discussed in more detail below. All other contract terms, including whether the option is a put or a call, the expiration date and strike price, are standardized. The premium is negotiated competitively in the trading pit on the floor of the exchange where the underlying futures is traded.

There is only one way to conceive the price mechanism of an option premium. If one jumps ahead to the expiration date (the last day it is traded), it becomes easier to understand. The only value that an option has at expiration date is the amount of money the holder could realize if the option was exercised. If there is no value to exercise on expiration date, the option is worthless.

How Intrinsic Value Affects Options

An option that would not be worthwhile to exercise has no intrinsic value. What, then, is the meaning of "intrinsic value"? Obviously it means that if a call option has a strike price below the futures price, it has intrinsic value. If you exercised it, you would be the owner of a futures contract (long) below the current price and the profit would appear in your account.

By the same line of reasoning, a put option has intrinsic value if its strike price is above the futures price. If the put option was exercised, you would have a short position in the futures at a price higher than the current quotation and the profit would appear in your account.

If a profit would not appear in the account, you would not exercise the option. If it has value, then the option is "in-the-money". In-the-money strike prices are more valuable than "out-of-the-money". If the underlying futures price is below the option strike price, and you exercised an out-of-the-money call option, you would find yourself with a long futures position at a level above current prices. You would have automatically created a loss in your account. A put option is out-of-the-money if the futures price is above the option strike price. The reasoning is similar. Exercise of the option would create a loss. An out-of-the-money option at expiration has no value and it will expire without being exercised.

There is a third category called "at-the-money" which means that the option strike price and the underlying futures price are identical. There is no reason to exercise an option when the strike price and the futures price are the same. If it was at expiration date, the holder would let it expire because it is worthless.

Exercise Price Compared with Futures Price

When	Calls are	Puts are
Futures price less than exercise price	Out of the money	In the money
Futures price equals exercise price	At the money	At the money
Futures price more than exercise price	In the money	Out of the money

At-the-money options have a demand based on the time left until expiration. All other factors being equal, an at-the-money option will command a bigger premium that an out-of-the-money option. If the other factors such as expiration date and strike price are the same, then the only other factor is time until expiration. Thus, besides intrinsic value, there is what is called "time value". Each option that is written has a certain amount of time before expiration. The buyers of the options (puts or calls) are willing to pay a certain amount of money (the premium) for a given option in anticipation that the underlying futures price will change enough to give the option (put or call) an increased value. The sellers or writers of such options will not undertake the risk without a premium that they consider worthwhile for the given period of time. By the expiration date, there is only intrinsic value; prior to the expiration date, there is time value.

How Time Value Affects Options

Time value is certainly a function of the time remaining until expiration and it also will reflect the volatility of the underlying futures price.

If the time remaining until expiration is a long period of time (measured in months), the premium would be higher. The best analogy is to think of it in terms of weather forecasting. It is easier to forecast tomorrow's weather than next month's. If it is easier to forecast, then the premium would be lower. The amount that an underlying futures contract may change in price concerns both the writers and buyers of options. Where there is reason to fear market volatility, sellers want higher premiums. Insofar as premiums compete with other instruments for investment, they also are affected by short-term interest rates.

Whatever the reasons are for premium values changing, it must be understood the prices themselves respond to supply and demand. If there are very few willing to write puts in a given situation, then the premium for puts will go up.

Should you decide to be a buyer of an option (either a put or a call), you must be prepared to pay the premium when the option is bought. That is the most that you can lose and is the amount of money that your FCM will want on deposit immediately.

If you should be the writer of options, you face the same risk as a participant in the futures market. If you had sold a call, and if the buyer of the call exercises his rights, you will be assigned a short futures position. Therefore, from the exchange's point of view, your risk is the same as someone who already has a short futures position. If you sold a put, your risk is the same as someone who already has a long futures position. Therefore, you will be expected to maintain adequate margin to cover potential losses on a day-to-day basis.

How Options Limit Losses

As with all other markets, speculators can choose from a variety of strategies depending on the risk they are willing and able to take. If a speculator in gold buys bullion anticipating inflation will drive prices upward, he has made a decision which time will prove or disprove. The gold was bought outright, which means interest on the money is lost and storage charges must be paid.

An alternative would have been to buy the same amount of gold futures in the most deferred month. The risk of a price decline compared to price increase is the same for the person with the futures position as for the owner of the bullion. The difference is the buyer of futures has only about 10% of the funds tied up in margin. The other 90% could be earning interest or put to use elsewhere, and no storage charges are incurred.

With the use of options on gold futures, the speculator has limited his losses to the cost of the call option and reduced his profits by the cost of the call option. The owner of the bullion and the long futures position holder are subject to almost unlimited losses if their judgement to be "long" gold proves to be wrong.

For example, suppose August 1985 gold call options with a strike price of $400 are available at $2,800 premium. Current futures quotations for that month are $370. If August 1985 future prices rose to $450 by June, the value of that call would be no less than $5,000. By selling the call back, the resultant profit would be $2,200. That is a return of almost 80% in just ten months, or an annualized rate of about 95%. Had gold prices remained unchanged, the loss would have been $2,800 to the call option buyer; and it would have been $7,000 in the long futures position. The bullion holder would find his assets reduced by $7,000 plus the cost of storage and interest.

The use of options limits your risk to the premium. As with futures, there are spreads or straddles that can be purchased. Writing them is even more complicated; however, the income from writing puts and/or calls is not to be ignored.

If one has sold puts or calls without having an offsetting position in the futures, it is "naked" or "uncovered" writing. It involves a high degree of risk in the event futures prices move against the writer.

There is less risk to those who write "covered" options. The reasons are not complex. Changes in the value of the premium for puts and/or calls will necessarily reflect the changing direction of the underlying futures price. Call options premiums will tend to decline in price as the futures decline; put options would increase under those circumstances. To be long futures and write calls is similar but not the same as being short the "cash" and long futures. The tendency of one to offset the other provides the element of protection with a suitable margin of profit that encourages option writing.

Options Strategies

There are several strategies which will allow the disciplined investor to assure himself of a "writing" profit. An investor may undertake a "buy and write" or "sell and write" strategy, depending on his view of the market.

If you believe that gold futures, for example, are not likely to decline over the next several months, a buy and write strategy is in order. To be more specific, the words "not likely to decline" mean prices may move upward but not very dramatically. Suppose it was June and December gold futures were about $350 per ounce. At-the-money December call options can be sold for $20 per ounce. The strategy would be to buy the December futures at the time the call option is sold. In effect, the writer has bought the futures at $350 and secured a selling price of $370 (purchase price plus premium). Where could such a strategy go wrong? If December futures declined below $340 (purchase price less premium), there would be an outright loss. Between the futures purchase price and $340 per ounce, market losses are covered by the premium for writing the call. If December futures rise above $370 per ounce, it is an "opportunity loss" as (with hindsight) more would have been earned by being outright long the futures.

The converse applies for sell and write strategies. Both were proposed with at-the-money options. There is a whole series of strategies of writing/buying out-of-the-money options which entails both covered and uncovered positions.

If an investor saw that the time premiums for puts and calls were temporarily distorted, he might sell a call, buy a put and the underlying future when the time premium on the call is greater than the time premium on the put.

In the preliminary material prepared by the Chicago Board of Trade (for options on soybean futures), certain option pricing models were used. In the table following, premiums were calculated with a $7 per bushel strike price. In this particular case, short-term interest rates were calculated at 9%. Bear in mind that a contract is 5,000 bushels. So the cost of the option must take that into account. Note that when the futures price is $7 per bushel, the strike price of $7 per bushel is "at-the-money". There is a difference in price between out-of-the-money puts and calls (the futures price being 40¢ higher or lower). It is the result of the various terms and the mathematics in the aforementioned model, but that variation is not important.

What is important is that when the futures price goes up (from $7 to $7.40), 30-day call options increase from $900 to $2,500. If the futures price decreases from $7 per bushel to $6.60 per bushel, 30-day put options will increase from $900 to $2,200.

Guide To Value

(Based of $7.00 per bu. strike price)

Days to Expiration		Futures Prices		
		$7.40	$7.00	$6.60
30	Call	$2250	$ 900	$ 250
	Put	225	900	2200
90	Call	2800	1550	750
	Put	800	1550	2700
180	Call	3300	2150	1300
	Put	1400	2150	3200
360	Call	4000	2950	2000
	Put	2200	2950	3850

The value of time is clearly indicated. Even out-of-the-money options increase in value as expiration dates move from one month to one year hence. The value shown in the table is only an illustration and is not to be construed as any pre-set value by the Board of Trade. Producers should be aware of these approximate costs when considering buying put options to protect themselves against declining prices. It is not only the cost of the option, but the total soybean production that has to be taken into account. With a yield of 30 bu. per acre, a farmer needs 167 acres, or about a quarter section, to produce 5,000 bu. of soybeans.

This need not exclude the average producer from the benefits of this new tool. It should suggest to the elevator owner ways of assuring his producer-clients of a minimum price while he undertakes to offset the risk by the use of options and futures. As an illustration only, it is possible for an elevator operator to point out to the producer that the current basis delivered to the elevator was 30¢ under the nearby futures. The farmer can accept the cash price (say $7.00 futures less .30, or $6.70) or he can "price later" which means the farmer is speculating on a rise in future prices. (The elevator operator presumably sold futures equalling the amount to be priced.)

Once the option market is functioning, the operator can give the farmer another choice. By reducing the basis by, say, 15¢ per bushel (this will be a competitive feature like the basis itself), to 45¢ under (or 6.55 in the illustration), the elevator will guarantee to the producer that $6.55 is the minimum that will be paid to him. If futures prices rise, the farmer's price will increase by the amount of increases to the day the farmer fixes price. If futures decline, the farmer will get no less then the minimum, in this case $6.55.

Some producers will be large enough to handle the options should they choose to do so. The elevator operator can provide the service, but in each case it is incumbent on the producer to decide what is best for him in the particular situation. For example, an outright sale at $6.70 will provide interest earnings (or debt reduction) from the day the funds are disbursed. At 12% annual interest, futures markets would have to increase by 22¢ the first month (15¢ discount plus 7¢ interest) for the farmer to break even.

It can be inferred that merchants may incorporate the opposite strategy by offering soybeans to buyers on a price-to-be-fixed basis that incorporates a minimum price. Any decline in futures prices would permit the buyer to "fix price" at the lower level. Thus, merchants may well be the buyers of puts and calls as well as the writer as they evolve the competitive strategies made possible by puts and calls, futures and basis and time. To sum up, producers, soybean crushers, elevator operators, like investors and speculators in gold, equities and debt instruments, can use options along with the futures market as a risk management tool.

14
Fifty Trading Rules Young Millionaires Use

Less than 25% of all futures speculators are successful. Yet, some speculators accumulate more than a million dollars in trading profits. What do the successful traders do differently? That's what prompted interviews with several young millionaire traders by *Futures* Magazine. Some of the rules the millionaires use are familiar to all traders; others may be contrary to common beliefs. "The most important factor is not what set of rules you use, but your discipline," noted one of the traders.

These are the trading rules that were generated from the interviews with the young millionaires:

1. *Use money you can afford to lose.* If you are speculating in futures with funds you need for some family project, you are doomed to failure because you won't be able to enjoy the mental freedom to make sound trading decisions, say the young millionaires.

Your futures speculation funds should be viewed as money you are willing to lose. Your position should be carefully analyzed so you don't jeopardize other funds or assets. One of the keys to successful trading is mental independence. "You've got to be able to trade with the minimum of 'static' or outside influencing factors, and that means your trading freedom must not be influenced by the fear of losing money you really have earmarked for a specific need," said one trader. "The marketplace is not the arena for 'scared money'," agreed another.

2. *Cut your losses short.* When the market moves against you, admit your mistake by liquidating your position. You can be successful if you are right on less than 50% of your trades if you keep your losses short and let your profits run. Some successful traders may have only three or four profitable trades out of ten, but, through discipline and stop loss orders, they get out early when they're wrong.

One of the most common failures of new traders is their inability to admit they're wrong, say the young millionaires. It takes a great deal of discipline to overcome the temptation to hang on to a loss, hoping the market will turn in your favor.

3. *Let profits run.* Cutting your profits short can be the cause of unsuccessful futures speculating. The slogan, "You never go broke taking a profit," doesn't apply to futures trading. The reason: Your losses will outweigh your profits unless you let your profits run. How do you know when to take a profit? Some of the technical rules on reversals and other chart formations can help. The successful traders say you should never take a profit just for the sake of a profit — have a reason to close out a profitable position.

4. *Know yourself.* You need an objective temperament, an ability to control emotions, to carry a futures position without losing sleep. Although trading discipline can be developed, the successful traders appear to be unemotional about their position. They suggest that people who can't control emotions look elsewhere for profits. "There are many exciting things happening in the market every day, so it takes a hard-nosed type of attitude and an ability to stand above short-term circumstances, or you'll be changing your mind and your position every few minutes," noted one of the millionaires.

5. *Start small.* Test your trading ability by making paper trades. Then, begin trading in small lots of 1,000 bu. to 3,000 bu. of grain at a time. Or, if your broker doesn't offer 1,000-bu. lots, start with a commodity like oats which is less volatile. Beginning traders should learn the mechanics of trading before graduating to more volatile futures.

6. *Don't overcommit.* Keep three times the money in your margin account that is needed for that particular position. Reduce your position, if necessary, to conform to that rule, say the traders. This rule helps you avoid trading decisions based on the amount of money in your margin account. If you are undermargined, you may

be forced to liquidate a position early at a costly loss that could have been avoided.

7. *Isolate your trading from your desire for profit.* Don't hope for a move so much that your trade is based on hope. The successful futures speculator is able to isolate his trading from his emotions. "Although hope is a great virtue in other areas of life, it can be a real hinderance to a commodity trader," said one of the traders interviewed.

When hoping the market will turn around in their favor, beginning speculators often violate basic trading rules.

8. *Don't form new opinions during trading hours.* Decide upon a basic course of action, then don't let the market ups and downs during the day upset your game plan. Decisions made during the trading day based on a price move or a news item are usually bad, say the successful traders. They prefer to formulate a basic opinion before the market opens, then look for the proper time to execute a decision that has been made apart from the emotion of the current market. When the speculator completely changes his direction during the trading day, it can confuse him and may result in generating lots of commissions with little profit.

9. *Avoid crowd psychology.* Successful traders like breathing room. When everyone seems to be long, they look for a reason to be short. Successful traders feel uncomfortable when their position is popular with the buying public, especially small traders. Periodic government reports on the position of traders of various sizes provide "overcrowding" clues.

Another clue is "contrary opinion." When most of the advisory services are long, for example, the successful trader gets ready to move to the sideline or to take a short position.

Some services give a reading on market sentiment determined by compiling opinions from many advisory services. If 85% of the analysts are bullish, it indicates an overbought situation. If less than 25% are bullish, it indicates an oversold condition.

10. *Block out other opinions.* Don't be influenced in your trading by every new opinion you hear. Once you have formed a basic opinion on market direction, don't allow yourself to be easily influenced. You always can find someone who can give what appears to be logical reasons for reversing your position. If you listen to these outside views, you may be tempted to change your mind, only to find later that holding your own opinion would have been more profitable.

11. *When you're not sure, stand aside.* Don't feel you have to trade every day or even hold a position every day.

The beginning trader frequently is tempted to trade or hold a position every day and that is a costly tendency. The successful traders develop patience and discipline to wait for an opportunity. After they have taken a position and begin to feel uncomfortable, successful traders either reduce the size of the position or liquidate.

12. *Try to avoid market orders.* Putting in an order to buy or sell at the market may show a lack of discipline, according to one successful speculator. To avoid violating this rule, he places specific price orders. For example, he says, "I want to buy 5,000 bu. of Dec. corn at $3.20."

However, there are times when he wants to liquidate a position immediately. Then the market order is helpful. Your goal should be to minimize the use of market orders, say the traders.

13. *Stay with active contract months.* In soybeans, for example, November, March, and July are usually the contracts with the highest volume and open interest, depending on the season. Trading these active contracts should enable you to get in and out of a position easily.

A similar caution should be noted for inactive futures. Low volume commodities are not the market for beginning speculators because it may be difficult to liquidate a position when you want to get out. Your broker will be able to help you in this area.

14. *Trade divergence between related futures.* Watch the "families": the grains, the meats or the metals. When you spot a wide divergence in a group, it could signal a trading opportunity. For example, if all grains except soybeans are moving higher, the young millionaires would look for an opportunity to sell soybeans as soon as the grains in general appear to be weakening. The reverse of this is true also. The traders would buy the strongest commodity in the group during periods of weakness.

15. *Don't trade too many commodities.* You'll hurt yourself if you try to have the necessary information and "feel" of several markets. Learn to know your limitations, and trade within these limits. Few traders successfully trade both metals and grains at the same time, because these two futures groups are moved by independent factors.

16. *Trade the opening range breakout.* This is a good price direction clue, particularly after a major report. A breakout of the

opening range may tell you the direction of trading for the day or the next several days. If the market breaks through the opening range on the high side, go long, say the millionaires. If it breaks out on the bottom side of the opening range, go short.

17. *Trade previous day's range breakout.* This rule is used by many successful traders who decide when to establish or lift a position. It means never buy until the price trades above the previous day's close, or never sell until the price trades below the previous day's close. Followers of a "market momentum philosophy" use this rule, believing that the weight in the market is in their favor when they wait for trading to break out of the previous day's trading range before adding to their position.

18. *Trade weekly range breakout.* This rule is similar to the daily rule, except it is used on weekly highs and lows. When the market breaks through a weekly high, it is a buy signal. When it breaks through the previous week's low, it is a sell signal.

19. *Trade monthly range breakout.* The longer the period you're watching, the more market momentum behind your decision. So, monthly price breakouts are an even stronger price trend clue and are vitally important for the position trader or hedger. When prices break out on the top side of the previous monthly high, it's a buy signal. When the breakout is on the bottom side of the previous monthly low, it's a sell signal.

20. *Build a trading "pyramid."* When you add a position, don't add more contracts at any one time than the number of contracts in your base commitment. Let's assume that your initial position was 20,000 bu. of soybeans. An ideal situation would be to pyramid by adding 15,000 bu., then 10,000 bu., then 5,000 bu., providing the market is moving your way.

The type of trading you want to avoid is the "inverted pyramid" where you add more than your original position on each additional trade. This is a dangerous trading technique because a minor market reversal can wipe out your profit for the entire position. Your average cost is closer to market price in the "inverted pyramid" situation, which makes you vulnerable. Another danger in pyramiding is overcommitting yourself to the point where you lack sufficient margin money.

21. *Establish your position at several prices.* If you want to be long 50,000 bu. of corn, you may want to do it in five installments of 10,000 bu. to see if the market is moving in your direction before

you become totally committed. Successful traders use the fundamentals and various technical signals to guide their trading, but the
most important key is market action. The young millionaires tend
to wait for the market to verify that the initial position was a good
one before putting on their full position.

22. *Never add to a losing position.* Regardless of how confident
you feel, if you establish a position that shows a loss, don't add to
it. It may mean that you are out of step with the market.

Some traders don't agree with this rule, believing in a "price
averaging" technique. The young millionaires interviewed believe
this can be a risky technique and a way to mentally justify adding to
a position that only magnifies a mistake.

This sometimes goes back to the "hoping" method mentioned in
Rule No. 7.

23. *Be impatient with losers.* Never carry a losing position more
than two to three days and never over a weekend, say the young
millionaires. This rule is used by one of the successful traders as a
way to force discipline. "Although it sounds very simple to say, 'Cut
your losses short,' it's a tough area even for seasoned traders," he
says. "That's why I make a flat rule for myself on carrying losses.
Over the last two or three years, blindly following this rule has
saved me from huge losses."

24. *Learn to like losses.* This rule says just the opposite of what
many traders think. One successful trader says, "Learn to like
losses because they're part of the business. When you gain the
emotional stability to accept a loss without hurting your pride,
you're on your way to becoming a successful futures speculator."
The fear of taking loss must be removed before you become a good
trader.

25. *Use stop orders cautiously.* The stop loss orders are easy
discipline. They may help you cut losses short automatically. An
important factor is to place your stop when you place your order. If
you don't, you're tempted to give the market a "few more cents,"
only adding to your potential loss. But remember, you should use
stop loss orders with great discretion because stops that are placed
too tightly can put you out of the market with a loss very quickly.
You can become "whipsawed" by poor placement of stops.

26. *Get out before maturity month.* The price of futures during
the delivery month may be more volatile, so the beginning trader
should move into other contract positions to avoid this added risk.

The profit potential in making and taking delivery is one that should be handled by the experienced cash market trader.

27. *Ignore "normal" seasonal trends.* Although the price of corn historically goes down at harvest, one of the young millionaires says he doesn't let that seasonal trend influence his trading. "Too many people try to trade seasonal trends, so I look for a place to do just the opposite," he suggests.

28. *Trade the divergence from normal.* This rule is one of the big keys some successful traders use regularly. They trade the divergence from normal or from what is expected. If traders in general believe the market is headed higher and the rally fails, it's usually a good sell signal, especially following government reports, according to one millionaire trader. He waits for market traders in general to lean one way, then times a trade in the opposite direction.

29. *Avoid picking tops and bottoms.* When you go against the trend, believing that the maket has either topped or bottomed, you are making yourself very vulnerable. This can be a very costly lesson to learn, say millionaires. They prefer to let the market price action prove that a top or bottom has been formed.

30. *Buy bullish news, sell the fact.* If market rumors are bullish, then you should buy on the news. But when the news reports turn into reality, then it is time to "sell the fact."

An example would be news of a potential grain sale. Because the market tends to "build the news into the market price," this rule would tell you to buy on the first piece of news; then when the sale was actually made, sell.

31. *Bull markets die of overweight.* There's an old stock market trading rule that says bull markets can fall flat of their own weight when prices get top-heavy. So, be especially sensitive to bearish news if you're long.

32. *Look for good risk:reward ratio.* Look for opportunities where the loss potential is small in relation to the profit potential. For example, if a future is trading near its recent historic lows, it could mean a long position has great upside potential in relation to possible loss. Or if it is trading just above government price support levels, there may be opportunity for a low-risk trade. Watching the trading range of a future over a year or several years helps you have the perspective to help determine the odds. Market fundamentals are also helpful in finding the "high odds" situation.

33. *Always take windfall profits.* Sometimes you take a position

and within 48 hours you have more profit than you ever expected. Rather than watching the market a few days to figure out why the profit came so fast, the young millionaires say, "Take quick profits and run!"

34. *Learn to sell short.* Most beginning speculators tend to be bulls, which means they buy markets that they think will go higher. Since markets often fall faster than they rise, you can frequently earn quicker profits by selling short, so it is good to learn to trade from the short side of the market.

35. *Act promptly.* The futures market is not kind to those who procrastinate. So the rule of thumb is to act promptly. This doesn't mean you should be impulsive, but if your judgement says you should liquidate a position, do it immediately.

36. *Avoid reversing your position.* When your position is a loser and you decide to get out, don't make a 180-degree turn. For example, if you have been long and decide the market is working against you, get out and stand aside for a while before going short. If you reverse a position, you can be whipsawed — losing as the market goes down, then losing more as the market moves up.

37. *Don't be a nickel and dimer.* If you want to be long, don't put a price order in 2¢ below the market, hoping to find a bargain. People who try to squeeze an extra penny out of the market frequently find the market moves almost to their target, then slips away. So, in hoping for an extra penny, they may give up a nickel. When you think it is time to do something, make your move.

38. *Take a trading break.* Trading every day dulls your judgement. One successful trader commented, "When I fall to 90% of mental efficiency, I begin to break even. Anything below that and I begin to lose." This trader takes a complete trading break every five or six weeks. If he has been successful, he goes to Florida. If not, he stays in Chicago.

A trading break helps you take a detached view of the market and tends to give you a fresh look at yourself and the way you want to trade for the next several weeks. "Sometimes you get so close to the forest you can't see the trees," said one trader. "A break helps me see market factors in better perspective."

39. *Know the price trend.* You can identify major price trends by using line charts, one of the fundamental tools of the successful futures trader. The mistake that speculators make is trying to buy or be long while markets are still in a basic downtrend or selling

short when they are in uptrends. Charting futures yourself or subscribing to a chart service can help avoid costly errors of selling into obvious uptrends and buying downtrends.

40. *Breakouts provide trading opportunities.* Some successful traders trade almost exclusively on this rule. They make bar charts. When prices break through a trendline and trade outside of the trendline for two or three days, it's usually a good trading signal. This violation of a downtrend line is also true for a sell signal when an uptrend line is penetrated. The trendlines then give you some guidelines for determing stops.

41. *Watch for 50% retracements of a major move.* You frequently hear the market is in a "technial reaction," which means that after a major move in either direction the market has a tendency to retrace up to 50% of that move. For example, if corn went from $2 to $3 in a major move up, then started to slide, the young millionaires would look for another chance to buy when the price dropped to $2.50.

42. *Use the half way rule when picking buy-sell spots.* This means finding out what range the commodity has been trading, then buying in the lower half of that range or selling in the upper half. This rule is particularly useful in a trading market or in a situation where the market is trading within a chart channel.

43. *Magnitude of market change forecasts trend.* When a market moves lower, but by a smaller amount each day, it may be a signal for an uptrend. When the market moves up each day, but in smaller amounts, it's an early signal that a downtrend may be just around the corner.

44. *Congestion areas form support or resistance.* These areas act as barriers that slow down price action. When you hear a market commentator say there is good technical support at a certain level, chances are good that he is looking at a line chart which shows an old congestion area where trading took place over a narrow range for several weeks. Major price moves may develop when the market breaks out of a trading area. Usually, the longer the market has been chopping arund in the trading area, the farther the price moves once it breaks out.

45. *Major moves frequently climax with a key reversal.* A key reversal of an uptrend is usually indicated when prices make new highs on high volume, then price erosion during the same day causes a lower close than the previous day's close. A key reversal of

a downtrend is a move to new lows, then a strong recovery during the day with a close higher than the previous day's close.

A key reversal may come in the form of a two-day reversal. On the first day the move is into new high ground and closes on strength. On the second day the market may open near the high close of the previous day, then closes sharply lower.

An island reversal is formed when prices gap into new highs on one day, then gap lower the next day.

46. *Trade head-and-shoulders formations.* When you observe a chart pattern that resembles a "head and shoulders," it is usually a sign the market is topping out. Upside down head-and-shoulders formations often signal a bottom. Head-and-shoulders patterns aren't obvious until the second "shoulder" is formed by a rally or sideways pattern.

47. *Prices usually move to fill gaps.* Future prices usually move to fill "gaps" formed in price charts. Assume the market closes Tuesday at new highs of $2.50. The next day it opens at $2.55 and moves higher, leaving a gap between $2.50 and $2.55. Eventually, prices are attracted lower to fill the gap.

48. *Sell triple tops; buy triple bottoms.* After a market has hit a peak the second or third time, it is a bearish signal. The reverse is true at the bottom. The young millionaires watch these signals and use them as a part of their overall trading strategy.

49. *Use volume for price clues.* When volume and price go up together, it's a buying signal. When volume increases and prices go down, it is a selling signal. But when trade volume goes down, regardless of price direction, it's a signal to stand aside or expect a market reversal.

50. *Open interest may tip off price trend.* If open interest increases as prices rise, it's a buying signal — especially if volume increases at the same time. The reverse is true also. If open interest increases with lower prices and on good volume, it is a selling signal.

15
Where Traders Get More Information

As your marketing expertise improves, you will demand more information from a wide variety of sources. This is not a complete list. But it gives you an idea of what you can get to start your information-gathering process.

Timely Information

Pro Farmer: A weekly newsletter for members of Professional Farmers of America. The letter and continuously updated hotline analyze current USDA reports and news developments on all major agricultural commodities. Written by a staff who know trading, *Pro Farmer* also makes specific marketing recommendations. *Pro Farmer* seminars are another good source of trading pointers. Professional Farmers of America, 219 Parkade, Cedar Falls, Iowa 50613.

Instant Update: Pro Farmer information available in an electronic newsletter, the first instant communication system for agriculture. Continuously updated price quotes, news highlights and weather and cash market information plus *Pro Farmer* analysis and recommendations. Requires a phone, regular television set and a special Radio Shack receiver unit. Professional Farmers of America, 219 Parkade, Cedar Falls, Iowa 50613.

Futures Magazine: The industry's only monthly magazine on futures trading. Monthly reports on pricing opportunities, major trading developments, hedging articles, charting guidelines and many other topics. *Futures,* 219 Parkade, Cedar Falls, Iowa 50613.

Corn/Bean Profit Alert: Weekly newsletter analyzing the fundamentals and technical aspects of both corn and soybean markets, including reports on supply and demand worldwide plus specific marketing recommendations. Professional Farmers of America, 219 Parkade, Cedar Falls, Iowa 50613.

PorkPro: The best timely information available on hogs, including retail and wholesale demand facts. Professional Farmers of America, 219 Parkade, Cedar Falls, Iowa 50613.

Doane's Agricultural Report: Weekly newsletter covering farm marketing and management ideas as well as production facts. "When to Sell and Buy" forecasts cover all major crops and livestock. Doane's Agricultural Report, P.O. Box 14351-B, St. Louis, Missouri 63172.

Farm Futures: Monthly magazine featuring section on price outlook and trading recommendations. Other articles detail individual markets, supply-demand prospects, charting techniques, etc. Market Communications Inc., 225 E. Michigan, Milwaukee, Wisconsin 53202.

Farmers Grain and Livestock: Weekly summary of agricultural news along with background reports and recommendations on how to market major farm commodities. Farmers Grain and Livestock, 1200 35th St., West Des Moines, Iowa 50265.

Kiplinger Agricultural Letter: Weekly coverage of all sectors of agriculture from a Washington perspective. Impact of USDA and Congress on farm prices is major focus. Kiplinger, 1729 H. St. N.W., Washington, D.C. 20006.

Washington Farmletter: Weekly letter concentrating on Washington's effect on farmers and farm prices. Washington Farmletter, 738 National Press Building, Washington, D.C. 20045.

Pork Industry Outlook: Biweekly newsletter covering hogs and factors like feed costs, government regulations, etc. relating to hogs and hog prices. Pork Industry Outlook, P.O. Box 1261, Welch Avenue Station, Ames, Iowa 50010.

Farm magazines: Many national magazines like *Farm Journal, Successful Farming, Progressive Farmer,* etc. and state magazines such as *Wallace's Farmer, Prairie Farmer,* etc. also present articles on trading and marketing. Although production schedules prevent magazines from being as timely as the telephone or newsletters, these magazines can still offer producers some good trading information.

Wall Street Journal and local newspapers: Daily open, high, low and closing prices are carried in most daily newspapers. You'll want to subscribe to at least one daily that gives commodity quotes.

Elevators: Many elevators have newswires feeding current information during the day.

Radio: Most radio stations carry periodic commodity price quotations. Find out what time they are broadcast in your area, then tune in to follow the market trend.

Telephone: Several good market services update your marketing knowledge any time, day or night. Professional Farmers of America updates information frequently during the day for members who call in on their market line.

Some state Farm Bureau organizations also have call-in services, giving a tape-recorded market summary each trading day. Some private firms, such as Comanco of Wyoming, also offer individual telephone consulting services.

In addition, several government sources provide telephone reports. Some universities, such as Iowa State University in Ames, provide capsule recorded highlights of major USDA crop reports. USDA also makes a daily telephone tape summarizing major happenings within the department during the day.

Commodity brokerage firms: Many brokerage firms have their own news and price networks and can provide you with the most timely information available. You can watch news and market quotes feed into an account executive's office, or you can call a local broker to get the latest price quotes from exchanges around the world.

A number of brokerage firms publish weekly newsletters and special reports which are sent to customers and prospects without charge. Many brokerage houses also have background information on futures markets and individual commodities available, and some present seminars or workshops for traders to learn more about trading commodities. Start with the firms nearest you, but don't settle for just any broker. Make sure your broker understands your trading goals and is able to work well with you.

The following list is not complete, but it does give you an idea of the commodity brokerage firms which can provide you with timely information and other trading assistance:

A.G. Becker Paribas Inc.
2 First National Plaza, Suite 2350
Chicago, Illinois 60603

Blunt Ellis & Loewi, Inc.
225 E. Mason Street
Milwaukee, Wisconsin 53202

B.C. Christopher Securities Co.
4800 Main Street
Kansas City, Missouri 64112

Clayton Brokerage Co. of St. Louis, Inc.
7701 Forsyth Blvd., Suite 300
St. Louis, Missouri 63105

Collins Commodities, Inc.
141 W. Jackson Blvd.
Chicago, Illinois 60604

Dean Witter Reynolds Inc.
Commodity Division Headquarters
150 S. Wacker Drive
Chicago, Illinois 60606

Drexel Burnham Lambert
60 Broad Street
New York, New York 10004

A.G. Edwards & Sons, Inc.
1 North Jefferson St.
St. Louis, Missouri 63103

Geldermann Peavey, Inc.
141 W. Jackson Blvd.
Chicago, Illinois 60604

Heinold Commodities, Inc.
250 S. Wacker Drive
Chicago, Illinois 60606

E.F. Hutton & Co., Inc.
One Battery Park Plaza
New York, New York 10004

Lind-Waldock and Co.
Chicago Mercantile Exchange Bldg.
30 S. Wacker Drive
Chicago, Illinois 60606

Merrill Lynch Energy Futures Group
777 W. Putnam Ave.
Greenwich, Connecticut 06830

Merrill Lynch Futures Inc.
2 Broadway
New York, New York 10004

McCormick Commodities, Inc.
135 S. LaSalle, Suite 2006
Chicago, Illinois 60603

Murlas Commodities Inc.
20 W. Monroe
Chicago, Illinois 60606

Paine, Webber, Jackson and Curtis, Inc.
140 Broadway
New York, New York 10005

Pioneer Commodities, Inc.
3150 Placida Road
Grove City, Florida 33533

Richardson Greenshields Securites, Inc.
4 World Trade Center, Suite 5274
New York, New York 10048

Rosenthal and Co.
141 W. Jackson Blvd.
Chicago, Illinois 60604

R. Rowland and Co.
100 N. Broadway, Eighth Floor
St. Louis, Missouri 63102

Shearson/American Express
2 World Trade Center
New York, New York 10048

Smith Barney, Harris Upham & Co., Inc.
333 W. 34th St.
New York, New York 10001

Stotler & Company
141 W. Jackson Blvd.
Chicago, Illinois 60604

Thomson McKinnon Securities, Inc.
One New York Plaza
New York, New York 10004

Wheat First Securities
P.O. Box 1357
Richmond, Virginia 23211

Charting Services

Commodity Perspective, Investor Publishing, Inc., 327 S. LaSalle St., Chicago, Illinois 60604. Over 60 computer-generated charts covering 26 commodities representing daily high, low, close prices; daily volume-open interest; 35 popular spread charts; contract high and low. Published Friday with Friday's closes; each chart 10″ × 13″; technical commentary every week.

Commodity Chart Service, Commodity Research Bureau, Inc., 1 Liberty Plaza, New York, New York 10006. Provides 200 weekly bar charts of daily price action in all major commodities traded in U.S. and overseas; charted daily trading volume and open interest; weekly technical comments; computerized trend analysis and commodity group price indices. Published each Friday after the close.

Commodity Price Charts, 219 Parkade, Cedar Falls, Iowa 50613. Comprehensive charts with five key price indicators combined on a single 11″ × 15″ page: bar chart, point-and-figure, moving averages, volume and open interest. Also, basis charts and spreads. Covers high-volume futures contracts.

Comtrend, Inc., 25 Third St., Stamford, Connecticut 06905. Mail subscriptions include bar, trendline, point-and-figure, spread charts and listings. Also life-of-contract data available with volume and open interest from 1960 in the form of bar, moving average, point-and-figure and spread charts. Write for sample kit.

The Professional Chart Service, Hadady Publications, 61 South Lake Ave., Suite 309, Pasadena, California 91101. Daily bar charts (11″ × 17″) depict 16 vital data. Completely drawn by computer including grids. Every contract month for 36 commodities available. Data plotted includes: openings, high, low, closing price, open interest and volume (total and individual contract month), cash price, key dates, 3- and 10-day moving averages, prior year's highs and lows, news evaluation, bullish consensus, commitment of traders and an evaluation of the fundamentals. Flexible weekly service permits selection of contract months for specific commodities.

Security Market Research, Inc., Dept. CM, P.O. Box 14096, Denver, Colorado 80214. Publishers of the SMR Commodity Service. Chartbook contains large technically-oriented charts of all major commodities. Each contract includes SMR Timing Indices. Mailed every Friday. Telephone service gives daily update of timing indices and recommendations.

Spread Scope, 17401 Stare St., Northridge, California 91325. Over 450 daily charts published weekly. Includes closing prices, spreads, basis charts, intermarket and intercommodity spreads, interest rates, currencies, open interest, volume, grain price ratios, feeding ratios, cattle-feeding profit margin, daily slaughter, bullish percentages, carrying charges. Also 20-day, 3-10 day, 5-20 day moving averages and differences.

General Background Information

Commodity Exchanges: Most commodity exchanges have free publications available which explain how your trade is handled, the role of the speculator and details on specific contracts. Exchanges also hold seminars aimed at increasing the level of trader knowledge on the use of commodity futures markets. Be sure to state your specific interest in asking for information.

Chicago Board of Trade
141 W. Jackson Blvd.
Chicago, Illinois 60604

Chicago Mercantile Exchange
30 S. Wacker Drive
Chicago, Illinois 60606

MidAmerica Commodity Exchange
444 W. Jackson Blvd.
Chicago, Illinois 60606

Board of Trade of Kansas City, Missouri, Inc.
4800 Main St., Suite 274
Kansas City, Missouri 64112

Commodity Exchange, Inc. (Comex)
4 World Trade Center
New York, New York 10048

Minneapolis Grain Exchange
150 Grain Exchange Bldg.
Minneapolis, Minnesota 55415

New York Futures Exchange
20 Broad St.
New York, New York 10005

Coffee, Sugar & Cocoa Exchange, Inc.
4 World Trade Center
New York, New York 10048

New York Cotton Exchange
4 World Trade Center
New York, New York 10048

New York Mercantile Exchange
4 World Trade Center
New York, New York 10048

Winnipeg Commodity Exchange
360 Main St.
Winnipeg, Manitoba R3C 3Z4, Canada

A visit to the commodity exchange will help you understand how trading is actually transacted.

Universities: Most land-grant colleges or universities have some courses and publications available on futures markets. Write to the Agriculture Economics Department at your nearest land-grant institution.

Books: Several publishers specialize in books for the hedger and commodity trader. For a listing of current books available and prices, write these publishers:

Investor Publications
Box 6
Cedar Falls, Iowa 50613

Commodity Research Bureau, Inc.
One Liberty Plaza
New York, New York 10006

Commodity Research Institute
Box 1866
815 Hillside Rd.
Hendersonville, North Carolina 28739

Dow Jones-Irwin
1818 Ridge Rd.
Homewood, Illinois 60430

Lambert-Gann Publishing Co.
Box 0
Pomeroy, Washington 99347

Traders Press
P.O. Box 10344
Greenville, South Carolina 29603

John Wiley and Sons
605 Third Ave.
New York, New York 10016

Windsor Books
Box 280
Brightwaters, New York 11718

USDA Reports

The U.S. Department of Agriculture issues hundreds of reports, newsletters and bulletins each year and provides taped telephone messages in many commodity areas each day. The following is only a partial list of information available from USDA:

Crop Reporting Board Catalog
Crop Reporting Board Calendar
Details of 475 reports issued annually on production, inventories, etc. of crops, livestock and other commodities. Write: Crop Reporting Board, USDA, Washington, D.C. 20250.

Situation and Outlook Reports
Situation and Outlook Calendar
Four or five reports each year on the following subjects of interest to futures traders: Livestock and meat, poultry and egg, fats and oils, sugar and sweeteners, cotton and wool, wheat, feed, agricultural finance, fertilizer, agricultural exports and world agriculture. Write: Economics Publications, ESCS, USDA, Washington, D.C. 20250.

Farmers' Newsletters
Newsletters in five commodity areas — wheat, feedgrains, live-

stock, soybeans and cotton — and a sixth on general agricultural topics. Identify which letter you want and write: Farmers' Newsletters, USDA, Washington, D.C. 20250.

Farmers Newsline
One-minute tape of latest crop, livestock and farm economic information available 24 hours a day. Call toll-free: (800) 424-7964.

Weekly Weather and Crop Bulletins
Summary of weather and its effects on crops and fieldwork progress the previous week by states. Write: Agricultural Weather Facility, USDA, Washington, D.C. 20250.

ESCS Research Abstracts
Monthly list and summary of recently published research reports. Write ESCS Publications, USDA, Washington, D.C. 20250.

Information Contacts
Booklet giving names and phone numbers of Economics, Statistics and Cooperatives Service experts in each commodity area plus list of state statisticians. Write: Information Division, ESCS, USDA, Washington, D.C. 20250.

How to Get Information from the U.S.
Department of Agriculture
Listing of information sources in USDA's Office of Governmental and Public Affairs and its agencies. Write: News Service, Office of Governmental and Public Affairs, USDA, Washington, D.C. 20250.

Federal-State Market News Reports, A
Directory of Services Available
Facts About Instant Market News
Taped telephone reports on prices, supply, demand and other market factors for grain, livestock, poultry, cotton and other commodity markets available 24 hours a day. State and federal agricultural departments cooperate on getting and transmitting information. For a list of commodities covered and phone number in each state, write: Information Division, Agricultural Marketing

Service, USDA, Washington, D.C. 20250.

Seminars: Universities, vocational-technical schools, ex-changes, the Futures Industry Association and several other sources offer classroom and correspondence courses in futures trading. In addition, state extension services, exchanges, bro-kerage firms, advisory services and other firms offer shorter, con-centrated seminars on trading and marketing techniques. Included in this list are:

Professional Farmers of America Institute. Presentations by some of the top authorities in the country range from the beginner level to the advanced trader. For details, write to Professional Farmers of America, 219 Parkade, Cedar Falls, Iowa 50613.

Commodities Education Institute. A week-long course designed primarily to train brokers and prepare them for the national com-modity examination, this course could also help the trader get a better understanding of futures markets. Complete course starts with the basics. For details, write Commodities Education In-stitute, 219 Parkade, Cedar Falls, Iowa 50613.

Government Regulatory Assistance

The Commodity Futures Trading Commission, 2033 K Street, N.W., Washington, D.C. 20581, is the major regulator of all com-modity futures markets although state agencies do have control over commodity pools and some other aspects of futures trading.

Regional offices:
Central region headquarters
  233 S. Wacker Drive, Suite 4600
  Chicago, IL 60606
  (312) 353-9499

Central region sub-office
  510 Grain Exchange Bldg.
  Minneapolis, MN 55415
  (612) 725-2025

Eastern region headquarters
1 World Trade Center
New York, NY 10048
(212) 466-2067

Southwest Region headquarters
4901 Main St., Room 208
Kansas City, MO 64112

Western region headquarters
2 Embarcadero Center, Suite 1660
San Francisco, CA 94111
(415) 556-7503

CFTC Hotline numbers:
48 states
(800) 424-9838
Alaska, Hawaii
(800) 424-9707
Washington, D.C.
254-7837

CFTC Publications:
Commitments of Traders in Commodity Futures, with
Market Concentration Ratios (monthly) (Chicago
office for Chicago markets, New York office for New
York markets)

On-Call Positions in Spot Cotton (weekly)
(New York office)

Stocks of Grain in Deliverable Position
(weekly) (Chicago office)

Index